Trust on the World Wide Web: A Survey

Trust on the World Wide Web: A Survey

Jennifer Golbeck

University of Maryland
College Park
MA 20742
USA
jgolbeck@umd.edu

the essence of knowledge

Boston – Delft

Foundations and Trends® in Web Science

Published, sold and distributed by:
now Publishers Inc.
PO Box 1024
Hanover, MA 02339
USA
Tel. +1-781-985-4510
www.nowpublishers.com
sales@nowpublishers.com

Outside North America:
now Publishers Inc.
PO Box 179
2600 AD Delft
The Netherlands
Tel. +31-6-51115274

The preferred citation for this publication is J. Golbeck, Trust on the World Wide Web: A Survey, Foundation and Trends® in Web Science, vol 1, no 2, pp 131–197, 2006

ISBN: 978-1-60198-116-5

Editorial Scope

Foundations and Trends® in Web Science will publish survey and tutorial articles in the following topics:

- Agents and the Semantic Web
- Content Management
- Databases on the Web
- Data Mining
- Dependability
- Emergent behaviour
- Human-Computer Interaction
- Hypertext/hypermedia
- Languages on the Web
- Mobile/pervasive
- Multimedia
- Network infrastructures
- Performance
- Scalability
- Security
- Semantic Web — metadata, ontologies
- Standards
- Trust and Provenance (Policy)
- Universal Usability
- User Interfaces
- Web Searching/Information Retrieval
- Web Services

Information for Librarians

Foundations and Trends® in Web Science, 2006, Volume 1, 4 issues. ISSN paper version 1555-077X. ISSN online version 1555-0788. Also available as a combined paper and online subscription.

Foundations and Trends® in
Web Science
Vol. 1, No. 2 (2006) 131–197

DOI: 10.1561/0400000006

now
the essence of knowledge

Trust on the World Wide Web: A Survey

Jennifer Golbeck

University of Maryland, College Park, MA 20742, USA, jgolbeck@umd.edu

Abstract

The success of the Web is based largely on its open, decentralized nature; at the same time, that allows for a wide range of perspectives and intentions. Trust is required to foster successful interactions and to filter the abundance of information. In this review, we present a comprehensive survey of trust on the Web in all its contexts. Three main targets of trust are identified: content, services, and people. Trust in the content on the Web, including webpages, websites, and Semantic Web data is addressed first. Then, we move on to look at services including peer-to-peer environments and Web services. This includes a discussion of Web policy frameworks for access control. People are the final group, where we look at the role of trust in web-based social networks and algorithms for inferring trust relationships. Finally, we review applications that rely on trust and address how they utilize trust to improve functionality and interface.

Contents

1

Introduction

Almost since the inception of the web, trust has been a concern. The success of the web is based largely on its open, unmanaged nature; at the same time, that allows for a wide range of perspectives and intentions. It provides access to billions of web pages with staggering amounts of information; as a communication medium, the web connects people and services to one another for exchanging information and making transactions; some of the most exciting new activity on the web is social, with social networks and collaborative interaction. In all of these cases, there must be trust to foster successful interactions and to filter the abundance of information.

There are three major challenges to using trust on the web.

- Trust management: Jøsang et al. [28] define trust management as *The activity of creating systems and methods that allow relying parties to make assessments and decisions regarding the dependability of potential transactions involving risk, and that also allow players and system owners to increase and correctly represent the reliability of themselves and their systems.* More generally, trust management is the

process of determining who has access to what information or resources in a system, identity management, and delegation of trust. Essentially, instead of simply encrypting data for its protection, trust management establishes a set of policies and determines the credentials of a person or services to access the data [17]. Doing this accurately and efficiently in a variety of domains requires many approaches.
- Computing trust: The known trust relationships on the web are only a small fraction of the potential pairings. Furthermore, the number of pages, services, and users on the web is so large, that it is difficult to estimate how much trust there is between entities. For example, a user cannot possibly know how much to trust every other user and every page on the web. Instead, trust must be calculated from other available data. Depending on the context, the methods for doing that will vary.
- Applications using trust: Managing and computing trust are interesting problems, but ultimately they exist to provide trust information that can be *used*. Trust in people or content provides insight into how they should be treated within a system (e.g., should a person be given access to a resource or how much weight should a user give to some information). Building applications that take advantage of trust information and improve their functionality because of it requires an understanding of how trust relates to the system's goals and how to integrate it. Doing this effectively is a challenge in all domains.

The proper way to address these challenges varies based on the context. For example, computing trust among web services via access control policies is quite different than computing trust between users in a social network. In this review, we consider trust in three domains: trust in content, trust in services, and trust in people. Once we have reviewed methods for managing and computing trust in those domains, we move on to applications. These integrate techniques from the domains to use trust for creating new functionality.

Trust has many meanings in computing, so we begin by describing the scope of this review with respect to the term. That is followed by brief descriptions of each section.

1.1 Scope of Trust

Within computer science, trust has been co-opted by many subfields to mean many different things. It is a descriptor of security and encryption [62]; a name for authentication methods or digital signatures [9]; a measure of the quality of a peer in P2P systems [96]; a factor in game theory [82]; a model for agent interactions [56]; a gauge of attack-resistance [104]; a component of ubiquitous computing [95]; a foundation for interactions in agent systems [13, 77]; and a motivation for online interaction and recommender systems [3]. On the web, many of these variations on trust are relevant. In a distributed, anonymous system like the web where services and information come from different sources, trust is especially important.

In this review, we treat trust as a concept that helps users (and agents) to make subjective decisions about content, services, or people when there is uncertainty. The breadth of these subjects excludes any single definition of "trust." The subjective component, however, excludes cryptologic and many security issues from our scope.

Trust is largely a social concept, and its sociological and psychological attributes have been studied extensively. That work is largely relevant to the study of trust on the web, and it informs much of the research presented here. However, this review is scoped to focus on the science of trust on the web, and particularly computing with trust. We introduce algorithms, standards, and empirical studies as primary results, and social research only as it supports the computational work.

Trust has been an important topic in the agents community. While agents are often studied on the web, the research into trust and agents applies equally to non-web agents. This research is certainly applicable to many web contexts, but we have scoped this review to cover web trust only. Thus, agent-based trust is outside of what we cover in this review.

1.2 Trust in Content

The web is its content. It has revolutionized the way people access information, and the amount of information they have access to. It has done this by providing billions of pages on every conceivable topic, and tools like search engines have made it accessible. On top of pages, there are vast amounts of data stored in databases and XML formats. The success of the web is due largely to the fact that there is no centralized control of the web; anyone can say anything. At the same time, this lack of moderation raises the question of trust with respect to content. Instead of being able to make a simple trust decision about one central editor or moderator, the user has to make a series of decisions each time she accesses a page. Which pages and what data can be trusted? How is that trust established? How is information about its trust shared? Section 2 looks at questions of trust in content, from web pages to data on the Semantic Web.

1.3 Trust in Services

Automated services are an important part of the web. Peer-to-peer (P2P) systems and web services are both widely used and important. Trust is important in this context because sensitive information is often exchanged between services, and also because users rely on their successful completion. Since the interactions between these services is usually automated, the conditions for trust must be established ahead of time by the users.

In Section 3, we look at trust in P2P systems and web services. The main issues addressed are how to judge trust based on performance, how to propagate trust assessments in distributed environments, and how to specify policies that increase the trust in web services.

1.4 Trust in People

The web is a social environment, facilitating the exchange of ideas, documents, money, and goods. The social components are becoming increasingly visible. Social Networking is one of the largest movements on the web, with hundreds of millions of user accounts among hundreds of different networks. Online communities supply a forum for discussion, ratings, and interaction. On the web, social trust and reputation are important factors that inform decisions about what to reveal to others and how to treat the information they provide. However, the web is also a very big place. The background information necessary for judging how much to trust an unknown person is often distributed and potentially private. Thus, methods for understanding, managing, computing, and applying trust are required.

Ultimately, users benefit from these social rankings because they can be used to judge things like the quality of information or the risk of a transaction. We can already see places where users have come to rely on trust and reputation, such as in eBay's feedback or rating websites like Epinions. There is more that can be done with social trust, but it requires a better understanding of the properties and dynamics of the relationship. Trust is not a new concept in computing; it has been studied as a facet of security, encryption, authentication, and quality. Trust as a *social* relationship, however, has very different properties. Because they are social concepts, trust and reputation are fuzzier concepts than are normally treated by computer scientists. The social behavior of web users and the scale of web systems require new understanding and computational techniques. At the same time, the growth and evolution in the way the web is used demands solutions that rely on these advances.

The emergence of recent work to better understand the computational properties of social trust and reputation is timely and necessary. Researchers have been making progress on all fronts. We have developed new theories for managing and for understanding the properties of social trust and reputation relationships. That has laid the foundation for the many algorithms have recently been developed for computing trust relationships between people. Analysis of reputation systems have also led to results that help protect against deception. As this grounds for assessing trust and reputation has improved, a number of new applications have been developed that utilize trust. This brings the benefits of understanding the user's social relationships into the applications that they already use.

2

Trust in Content

One of the first decisions a web user must make is whether or not to trust the information they are seeing. In its simplest form, that means determining the trust a person should have in information on web pages. On the Semantic Web, the metadata layer of the web, trust is the highest goal. The interrelationships among data and people become a source of information about trust. In this section, we look at early work on trust in web pages, and then move on to the Semantic Web where building trust in content is an ultimate goal.

2.1 Trusting Web Pages

Web pages are what most people would identify as the basic unit on the web. When users visit websites, they must decide whether to trust the content, or whether to engage in a transaction. In the late 1990s and early 2000s, much work was conducted to understand what encouraged users to trust web sites. Much of the attention was focused on trust in e-commerce websites, as the need for trust is much greater since money is involved [34, 90, 91, 99, 109].

In [28], the authors identify three factors that impact trust in online environments: perception of credibility, ease of use, and risk. Earlier results on user trust in e-commerce support this. In [23], a large study of users and e-commerce websites identified six major features that encouraged trust in websites. The first two items deal with outside reputation, while the last four are specific to the design and implementation of the website. All six address some aspect of the factors from [28]:

- Brand: The reputation of a company independent of their website affects users' trust and thus willingness to do business with the website.
- Seals of Approval: Icons from companies that certify a site as following security measures fosters trust from users.
- Navigation: If users have a difficult time navigating the website, they are less likely to trust it.
- Fulfillment: As a user goes through the order process, they develop (or lose) trust in the website from their experiences.
- Presentation: The design and presentation of information has a significant impact on how much a user will trust the website.
- Technology: The technologies used to create the website also impact the user's trust.

In addition to these aspects, the expected result is that trust is developed over time. The more users interact with a site, the more they gain information that will help them decide how much to trust it. Figure 2.1 illustrates the process of developing trust (specifically for e-commerce websites) as described in [59].

The work in [35] follows up on the results from this study, addressing what makes a website *credible.* They define credibility as believability; more credible sites are the ones users are more likely to believe. Credibility ties closely with trust, and the authors find that trustworthiness is a major component. Other factors affecting credibility include many of the same features as in [23].

In the definitions in [35], trustworthiness reflects well-intentioned, truthful, unbiased websites. Subjects in their study identified the

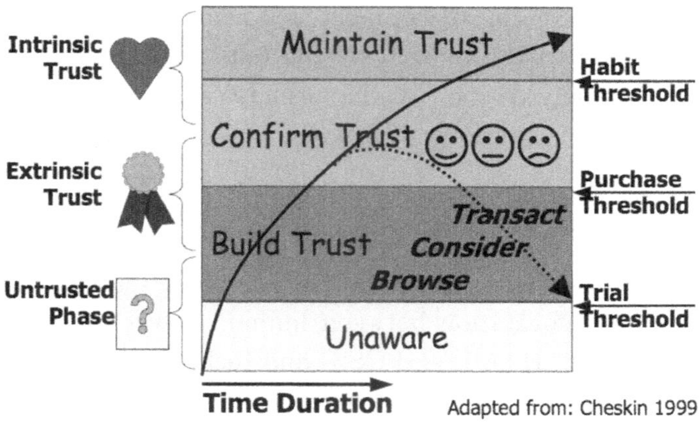

Fig. 2.1 An e-commerce trust transition model, taken from [59] and adapted from [23].

following factors as contributing to trustworthiness:

- Linking: Both where the user was linked from and where the site links to are important.
- Policy statement: Sites that stated a policy on content were more trustworthy.
- Social recommendations: If a friend recommends a site, users are more likely to trust it. This trend is repeated throughout this entire review.
- Business interest: This study was judging how much subjects could trust the content on a page. If the page was an independent organization rather than a for-profit company, users were more likely to trust its content.

These two reviews capture the core ideas that affect user's perception of how much to trust the websites. This kind of trust in content is largely visual and social — the design, perceived effort, and real world reputations of site owners and recommenders all impact trust. But what about when there is just data — information without a visual context or clear tie to a business or organization? For these situations, developing trust is more complex. To investigate the issue of trust in information content, independent of trust in the websites that host it, we will look specifically at efforts on developing trust in the Semantic

Web. While some of the technologies for Semantic Web trust do not translate directly to the hypertext web (such as the practice signing RDF graphs), many of the broader principles do apply to content in web pages and can be informative when building traditional content.

2.2 The Semantic Web

The web was originally conceived as a medium for the exchange of documents and information between humans. Over the last 15 years, the languages (e.g., HTML and CSS) and technologies (e.g., browsers) have evolved to improve the presentation to humans. However, this evolution has also made it more difficult for computers to find much of the content on the web. The Semantic Web (SW) is an extension of the current web, designed to represent information in a standard, machine-readable format.

Each object or "resource" on the web is given a unique identifier in the form of a Uniform Resource Identifier (URI). Ontologies are used for describing objects and their relationships to each other. A statement on the Semantic Web takes the form of a triple, which consists of a subject, predicate, and object. The subject is the resource being described, the predicate is the property or attribute of the subject, and the object is either another resource or a literal value. All three parts of the triple (except for literal values) are given by URIs. Because the URIs are used in these descriptions, or *knowledge models*, data can be stored anywhere on the web and referenced by its address. In effect, the web becomes a large distributed, collaborative database represented by a graph (where subjects and objects are nodes and predicates are edges).

The SW is built on knowledge representation languages based on XML, which are used to define ontologies that add structure and semantics to the data. The Resource Description Framework (RDF)[1] provides basic semantics, including the ability to define *properties*, which are the predicates in triples. RDF Schema (RDFS)[2] extends RDF with the semantics for defining hierarchies of classes and domain and range

[1] http://www.w3.org/1999/02/22-rdf-syntax-ns.
[2] http://www.w3.org/2000/01/rdf-schema.

restrictions on properties. The Web Ontology Language (OWL)[3] adds a much richer semantics including set operations, local domain and range constraints, enumerated classes, and equivalent and differentiated classes and individuals. OWL comes in three sub-languages. OWL Lite and OWL DL, which are formally aligned with Description Logics [12], and OWL Full which adds more expressivity.

The semantics of these languages allow a reasoner to infer connections among data. A simple example of an inference would be along a hierarchical relationship. If we know there is a class of things called Animal, a subclass of Animal called Human, and an instance of Human called Bob, we can infer that Bob is also an Animal. The logical inferences that an OWL reasoner would support on the Semantic Web can be much more complex. Rules can also be used to make inferences beyond the semantics supported in OWL.

As is shown in Figure 2.2, proofs and trust are the top two layers of the Semantic Web vision. Proofs are sets of rules that verify identity, access, or permissions based on a set of requirements. An agent demonstrates that it meets those requirements by providing a set of explicit or inferred statements on the web. Proofs can be a direct set of statements, but can also include the provenance describing how the proofs were generated. The role of provenance in building trust is described more in Section 2.4.

Trust is the top architectural layer, and trust is established through proofs that are believed. Trust has also taken on a richer meaning, referring more broadly to how trust can be established in data on the web, whether from logical proofs, social relationships, or other means. The fact that trust was included as a top priority of the Semantic Web from the very beginning indicates how strongly the standards groups, industry, and academia have come to understand the web is more than protocols and languages, and that their efforts must strongly consider the end use of web-based information.

Work on the trust layer of the SW has been interesting but fragmented, largely because of the varied set of views on what constitutes "trust." The first efforts on the Semantic Web began in the World

[3] http://www.w3.org/2002/07/owl.

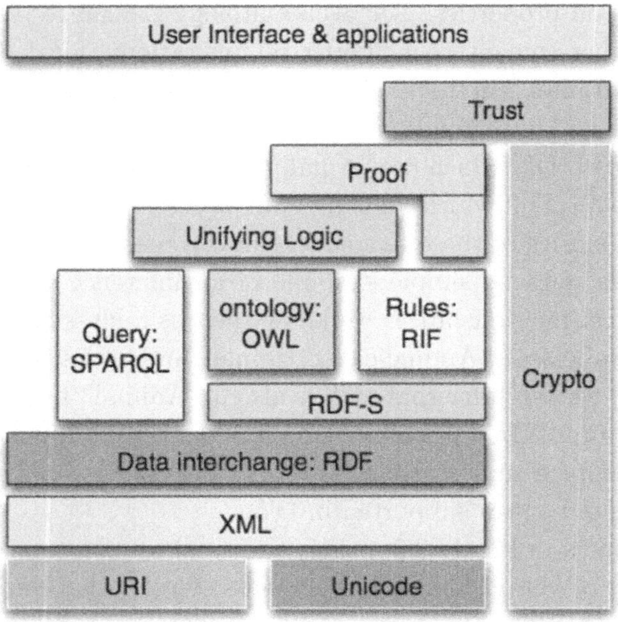

Fig. 2.2 The 2006 Layers of the Semantic Web, taken from [14].

Wide Web Consortium in 2001, and much of the work was on developing and standardizing the SW languages. This meant that there was not a coordinated effort on trust through the W3C, and instead researchers brought their own backgrounds to the problem. Digital signatures were viewed and explicitly stated as an important part of the SW and the trust layer, and there has been interesting work on authentication and digitally signing documents or graphs [20]. Work on policies also translated well to the SW domain, and the work on policies for access control are discussed extensively in Section 3. Policies for web services have been of particular interest, with SW technologies being used to describe the policies as well as the services. Languages for describing these policies, including WS-Trust [1], are also included in the discussion in Section 3. In parallel, work on social trust based on social networks on the SW was being investigated [47, 50, 81]. These different tracks of research on trust and the Semantic Web continue, indicating that the trust layer will really be interwoven with proofs, authentication/crypto, and applications. Rather than a coherent group effort on standardizing languages, algorithms, or techniques, it is likely that the different aspects of trust will be investigated along their own paths.

The "layer cake" shown in Figure 2.2 is the 2006 version, updated from an earlier structure that did not have the "user interface and applications" layer. The addition of this layer is important for the application of Semantic Web technologies to the web as a whole. The Semantic Web is not designed to be a front end application that users interact with directly. It is a set of knowledge management tools and technologies that will ultimately be used to support other applications. Since the knowledge is on the web, most of those applications will also be on the web in one way or another. Current examples applications supported by Semantic Web technologies include mSpace [93, 107], CS AktiveSpace [92], Foafing the Music [22], GroupMe! [4], and Chip Demonstrator [10] just to name a few. Because Semantic Web sets out to create *trusted* data, applications like these that are built on top of that data will naturally be using more trusted information. Thus, the techniques for building trust on the Semantic Web will ultimately build trust in the information that supports applications on the hypertext web.

Since it was introduced in 2001, applications that use Semantic Web technologies have been proliferating. We will see some of these in the rest of the review, particularly in the discussion of social networks — one of the largest uses of Semantic Web vocabularies — and web services. In this section, we will look at Semantic Web information systems with components designed to estimate trust in the data itself.

2.3 Trusting Semantic Web Information Sources

Yolanda Gil and Varun Ratnakar addressed the issue of trusting content and information sources with their TRELLIS system [38]. TRELLIS is a Semantic Web-based information analysis tool that supports collaborative annotation of sources. Documents, such as existing web documents or messages supplied by users, are indexed by the system. Then, users can add annotations to that resource which can be about the document directly, or about the person who created it and the context in which it was created. As users add annotations, they can include measures of Credibility and Reliability about a statement, which are later averaged and presented to the viewer. These annotations are available to anyone else using the system. Thus, users can assess the quality and how much to trust information based on the document and community annotations.

Another approach is to consider the trust for a collection of statements. The structure of information on the Semantic Web is a graph. Classes or instances are nodes and the relationships between them are edges. Making statements about these graphs on the Semantic Web is difficult because a graph is an abstract concept, not a named entity. In [21], the authors propose a small extension to the RDF and OWL foundations, allowing graphs to be named with a URI. This addition means graphs can be signed with digital signatures and referred to in other statements. From there, it follows that trust techniques can be applied to an entire graph. These could include annotation methods, such as those in the TRELLIS system, trust and provenance techniques as described in the next section, or a combination of approaches.

In [46], the authors present a mechanism that ties trust derived from social networks (discussed in depth in Section 4) to data asserted by those people. Allowing users' trust in the author as representative of their trust of a statement made by that author, users are able to filter statements in a Semantic Web knowledge base. The authors also discuss possible extensions of this type of filtering to inferred statements within knowledge bases. This work begins to touch on issues of data provenance, which we discuss throughly in the next section.

2.4 Provenance on the Semantic Web

Provenance is the history of something; in computing, it is the history of data. Provenance systems allow users to verify data, repeat analyses, and discover dependencies. Knowledge about provenance helps users verify the authenticity of data and decide how trustworthy it is.

It is particularly of interest in systems where the interconnections between data are important for judging its quality. In a sense, provenance is designed to build trust. Knowing the history of data and the relationships among it can help users judge how much to trust the content. Provenance also can describe who created data, leading to the use of social relationships to judge how much trust should be placed in the data.

The ability to automatically trace the dependencies between data back to the source requires support within a system. On the web, the Semantic Web is a natural fit for representing provenance, as it contains explicit support for representing and inferring connections between data and processes, as well as for adding annotations to data.

There are many widely different approaches to representing provenance and interacting with it, but some of the benefits offered by Semantic Web techniques were presented in the Provenance Challenge [84]. The challenge was designed to provide an application and set of tasks that served as common ground for comparing provenance techniques. It used a scientific workflow based on a series of transformations over functional MRI images (see Figure 2.3). Participants were instructed to represent whatever information about the process they saw fit, and to answer a series of sample queries over the data.

There had been some work on using Semantic Web technologies to represent provenance in scientific workflows [113], and of the 17 submissions to the Provenance Challenge, four used RDF or OWL for representing data [65], [36], [112], and [45]. That includes three of the six teams who successfully answered all the challenge queries. While the Provenance Challenge is a very specific example, it is designed to test the systems' capabilities for working with provenance, and the participants have demonstrated that Semantic Web reasoning and querying can be effective methods for handling provenance.

With provenance on the web, the next step is using to judge how much information should be trusted. That determination can be made by a user or automatically through sets of rules. For example, if someone discovers that one of the original files used in a scientific workflow was corrupted, they can mark any derived files or conclusions drawn from those files as untrustworthy. In an intelligence system, where raw

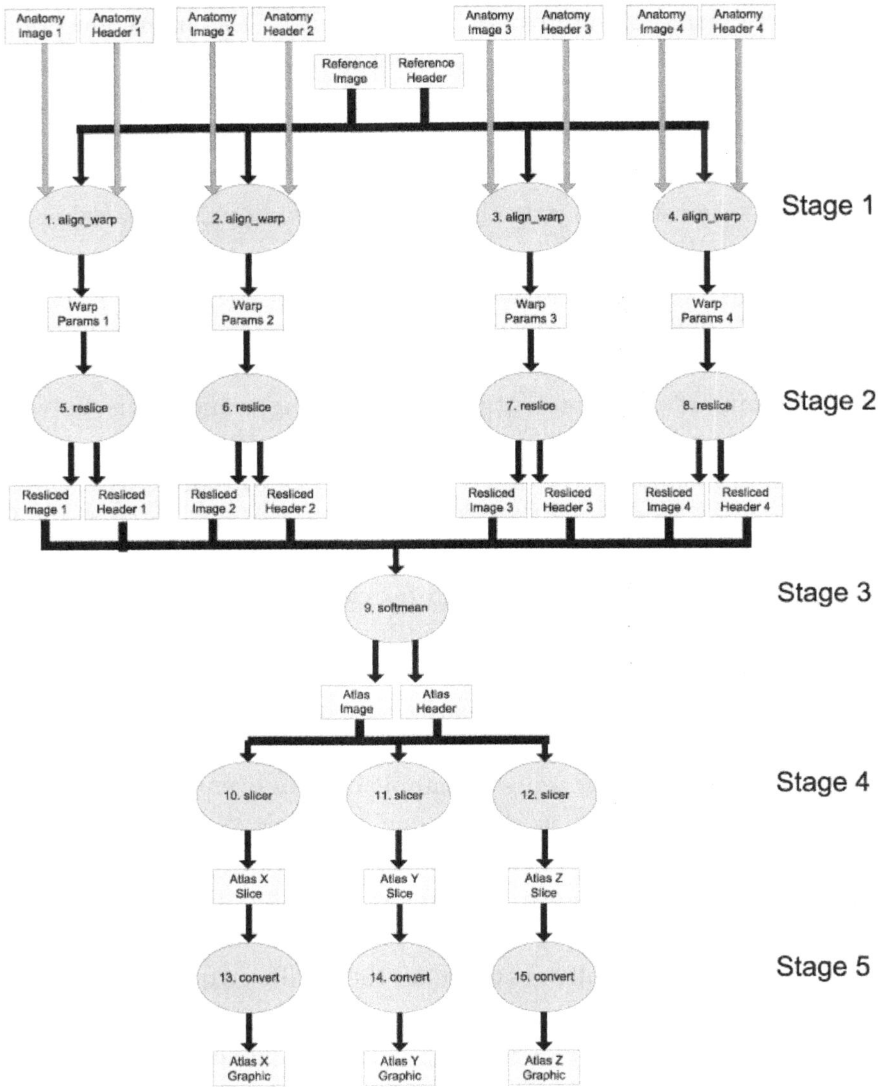

Fig. 2.3 The Provenance Challenge workflow. Each box represents dat and each oval represents a process.

intelligence is analyzed and conclusions become part of the knowledge base, a user may decide that a particular conclusion was incorrect, and would then mark any knowledge that depend on that conclusion as untrustworthy.

Social factors can also be tied in to these systems. Provenance also connects data to the people who created it. The authority, reliability, and trustworthiness of the person who created information can be used to judge the information itself. Some early work discusses the trust and provenance in the information retrieval space [76]. Though written before the emergence of web-based social networking, it eludes to the potential for using them. Via a "web of vouching" — essentially a social network with trust — the review presents the idea of using social relationships to decide how much to trust information according to who created it. Since social networks are also a prominent application on the Semantic Web (see Section 4.1.2), they can be directly integrated with provenance.

2.5 Conclusions

In this section, we have looked at issues of trust in content on the web, specifically data on the Semantic Web. Since its inception, trust has been a critical part of the Semantic Web vision. We have reviewed research on trusting statements generally as well as in the context of provenance. As some of these papers have suggested, trust in content can follow from trust in the people who created it. Furthermore, the web is more than just content; services are an important part of it. It is these two issues — trust in services and trust in people — that we address in the next two sections.

3

Trust in Services

The most popular perception of Peer-to-Peer (P2P) is as file sharing systems where people can download free music and videos. In these cases, trust and reliability are less important because users pay nothing for the service and get files for free that they might otherwise have to pay for. However, in business applications where users are paying to access information provided by P2P systems or web services, the services must be secure and reliable. This requires methods for authentication, authorization, determining quality of service, and sharing this information. For a P2P system or web service network to work, each node must correctly implement the network protocols and provide access to uncorrupted files. If a node is not reliable, it can degrade the usefulness of the entire network. Thus, the trust in a node can be estimated with respect to how well it participates in the network, and that is determined by aggregating data about many individual interactions.

Determining and managing trust in peers or services is a challenging problem; it requires a system that can scale and handle the distributed nature of the entities. In this section, we will look a trust management, algorithms for computing trust in P2P systems, and efforts for encoding trust in web services.

3.1 Trust Management

Khare and Rifkin [63, 64] present the issue of trust management as asking the question "Is someone trusted to take some action on some object?" On the web, people or agents interact with services, and the services also interact with one another. P2P environments and web services are two example domains where trust can be especially critical, and in this section we look at trust management in these domains.

When P2P or web service environments grow large enough to be interesting, managing trust becomes a difficult problem. The probability of interaction between two peers or services (call them nodes in the network) grows smaller as the network grows larger. Thus, it is unlikely that nodes will have any information about most others. If each node were to broadcast data about its interactions, it would add a tremendous overhead to the network. Generally, the network will also be too big for each node to maintain information about the trust of every other. A centralized service that collects, computes, and provides trust information about other nodes in the network is one solution, but that does not scale in large distributed systems. Furthermore, while a centralized system is effective, it requires disclosure of identity that some users may find unacceptable; a distributed system allows for greater anonymity, though with increased risks of identity hijacking [78].

In the P2P space, the most basic trust management systems involve polling. Each node keeps a record of its transactions with other peers, and a rating of the trust in its partners. When a node wants to discover a rating for an unknown peer, it broadcasts a request for information. The node's neighbors then propagate the request to their neighbors, and so on until a time limit is reached. This is the basis of the approaches used in [27] and [29]. These methods can be effective, but they require much bandwidth and computing power. As such, they were followed-up by management systems and search methods designed to be more efficient with respect to the network.

A decentralized approach to trust management in P2P systems is presented by Aberer and Despotone in [6], where each node is assigned a subset of trust ratings to store. In their system, a peer can register a complaint if it has a bad transaction with another. To guard against retaliatory complaints, reputations are determined by the product of complaints against the node and complaints registered by the node. To store this data in a way that all nodes can access it, the system uses aP-Grid [5], where each node is associated with a path of a virtual binary search tree with depth two. Nodes store complaints about nodes for which the associated path corresponds to the prefix of the data key, and a routing table allows a node to forward requests to other nodes in the network. Figure 3.1 illustrates a sample query for complaints about node 6, represented by the binary key 100. This system allows each node to only store a subset of the complaints, and the data can be duplicated (e.g., for path "00" in the figure), protecting against failures or fraud.

The NICE [96] system is a platform for cooperative distributed systems, and provides another example of distributed trust management for P2P systems. In contrast to the previous approach, each node stores

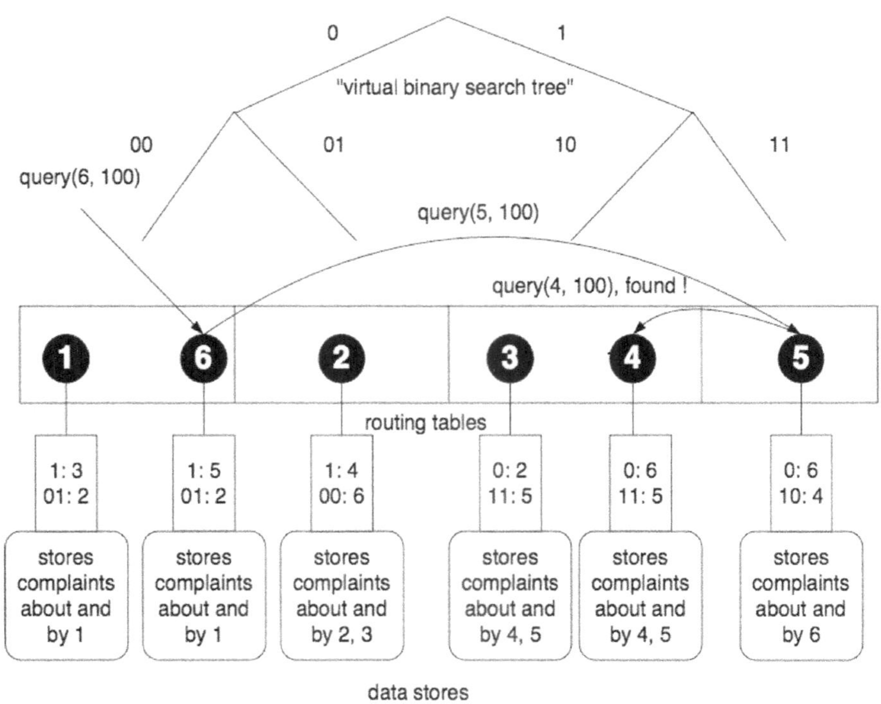

Fig. 3.1 Example of the P-Grid data management system, taken from [6].

the trust ratings assigned to it by others. When two nodes complete a transaction, an edge is added between them in the graph. Each node creates a signed statement (called a *cookie*) that describes the quality of a transaction with a real valued trust rating in the [0,1] interval. The partner in the transaction can store the cookie to prove to other nodes that is should be trusted later on. If a node (Alice) wants to use resources from another node (Bob), Alice can either present a cookie from Bob to prove that she is trustworthy, or, if there is no history between Alice and Bob, Alice can search for Bob's cookies in the network. She begins by seeing if any neighbors for which she has cookies have a cookie from Bob. If so, she can present Bob with two cookies: one from Bob to the intermediary, and one from the intermediary to Alice. This process is iterated, so Alice may ultimately present Bob with a set of cookies representing trusted paths from him to her in the network. Naively, this search can be highly inefficient, but effective P2P search structures can be implemented on top of NICE to make a better search. Once Bob receives this set of trust values, he can infer how much to trust Alice. Details on this trust inference algorithm are presented in Section 3.2.

BambooTrust [69] is a trust management system with a P2P architecture designed for large scale public computing platforms like the Grid. It is based on XenoTrust [32], a trust management architecture for the XenoServer project. XenoTrust has mechanisms for storing trust or reputation, and rules for sharing that in a distributed environment. XenoTrust maintains aggregated trust information based on rule-sets created by users. Because XenoTrust is designed for supercomputing environments, BambooTrust translates it to a distributed open architecture that is a better fit for public computing systems. On top of the XenoTrust model, BambooTrust adds an architecture for storing reputation in a distributed way and includes methods for retrieving that data.

On the web service side, [16] developed the idea of trust management as an alternative to authorization schemes. They present a language for writing policies that limit access to online resources, and for describing credentials that are used to gain access. These were embedded in *PolicyMaker*, and later in the *KeyNote* trust management system.

Applications define their own policies that outline the credentials necessary to access their resources. When a person or other agent attempts to use the application, they must provide proof that they satisfy the requirements of the policy. Applications make queries to a Keynote interpreter to verify if access should be granted (see Figure 3.2). This basic technique is used in more modern web service policy systems, discussed in Section 3.3.

A framework for decentralized trust management is also presented in [60]. The authors consider the task of authorizing users to access a web service in the system, the delegation of access (e.g., if a professor has access to a service controlling a projector in a classroom, that access can be delegated to a visitor who wants to project a presentation), and the data structures and ontologies to support that.

3.2 Computing Trust in Peer-to-Peer Systems

Trust management models describe how trust information is stored and shared in P2P systems. Once the information is collected about a node,

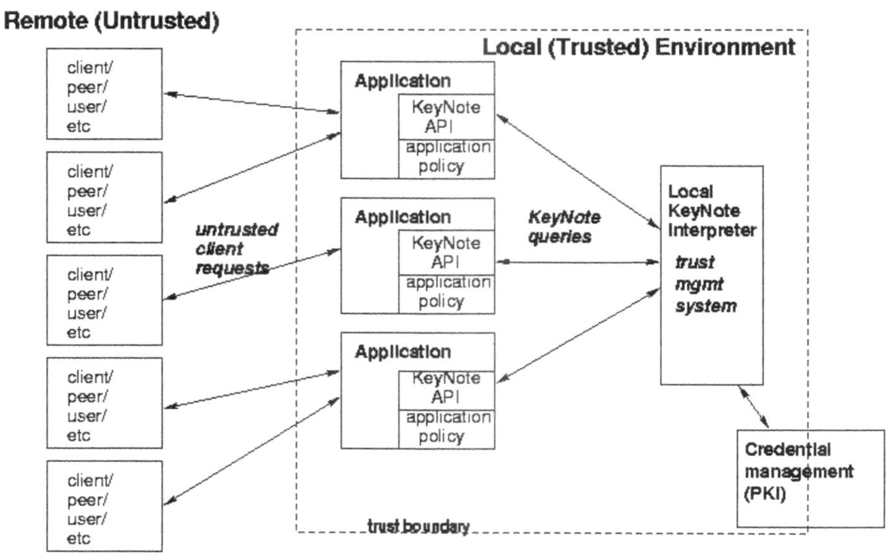

Fig. 3.2 The KeyNote trust management architecture. Remote agents connect to applications that rely on a Keynote backend to determine access to resources.

it must be composed into a recommendation of how much to trust the node. Methods for computing trust range from simple to advanced; it is important to note the separation of the trust management component from the trust computation component. A very advanced trust management system may use a simple average to *compute* trust from the collected values, and vice versa.

There is significant overlap between algorithms for computing trust in P2P networks and algorithms for computing it in social networks; many algorithms can be applied in either domain. In this section, we present the methods designed specifically for use in P2P networks, and Section 4 will present similar algorithms for social networks.

If trust is valued continuously in a range, the trust in a node can be computed as a simple average of the trust ratings assigned to it by its neighbors. The trust computation method in [6] uses a binary trust valuation. In that model, the trust computation is also straightforward; if a node is caught cheating by any node with which it interacts, it is marked as globally untrustworthy.

Yu and Singh [111] also uses a relatively simple scale for trust, with ratings as -1, 0, or $+1$. This model builds a social network among peers where edges contain the trust ratings between peers. Trust ratings (as well as changes in trust ratings) propagate through the network. To update node j's trust in node i (given by $T_j(i)$), it receives testimonies (E) from its neighbors. Each testimony is a product of node j's trust in its neighbor and the neighbor's trust in the next node on the path. For a path χ, the testimony that node j receives about node i is given by $E_j(i) = T_j(k)T_k(k+1)$. Node j then averages all the testimonies it received about node i and updates its trust value. At time $t+1$, the trust node j has in node i is given by $T_j^{t+1}(i) = T_j^t(i) - \overline{E}|T_j^t(i)|$ if the signs of $\overline{E}$ and T_j^t are the same, or $T_j^{t+1}(i) = T_j^t(i) + \frac{\overline{E}}{1-\min\{|T_j^t(i)|,|\overline{E}|\}}$. Essentially, at each time step the trust value is updated up or down according to the testimonies received, and how trustworthy the witnesses are.

In the NICE system [96], discussed in Section 3.1, nodes who have never interacted can infer a trust value based on paths in the network. Consider Figure 3.3 where Alice wants to know how much to trust

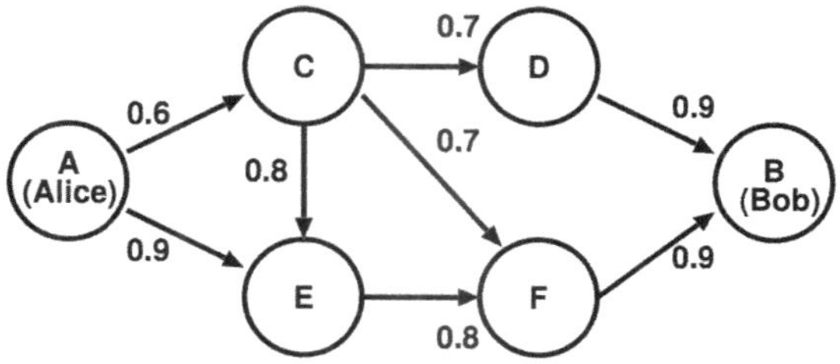

Fig. 3.3 A network with trust values indicating how much the source of the edge trusts the sink. Ratings are on a 0–1 scale where 0 is low trust and 1 is high trust. Taken from [96].

Bob. Two possible methods are offered for inferring a trust value. Alice could choose the strongest path, determined either by the path with the highest minimum value ($AEFB$ in the figure) or by the path with the highest product of all values on the path, and use the lowest value on that path as the inferred value for Bob. The other option is a weighted average of strongest disjoint paths. The weights in the average are given by Alice's trust in her direct neighbors. This system is robust in that it does not consider any trust value twice.

The EigenTrust algorithm [61] considers trust as a function of corrupt vs. valid files that the node provides. A peer maintains information about the trust is has in its peers with which it has interacted based on the proportion of good files it has received from that peer. For one peer to determine the trust it should have in another with which it has not interacted, it needs to gather information from the network and infer the trust. The EigenTrust algorithm calculates trust with a variation on the PageRank algorithm [88], used by Google for rating the relevance of web pages to a search. A peer creates a direct trust rating for another peer based on its historical performance. In its simple form, the algorithm uses a matrix representation of the trust values within the system and over a series of iterations it converges to a globally accepted trust rating of each peer. Because of safeguards built into the system, EigenTrust has been shown to be highly resistant to attack.

A Bayesian network-based trust model is proposed in [106]. In their system, each node maintains a small Bayesian network with information about different aspects of trust. Figure 3.4 shows an example where

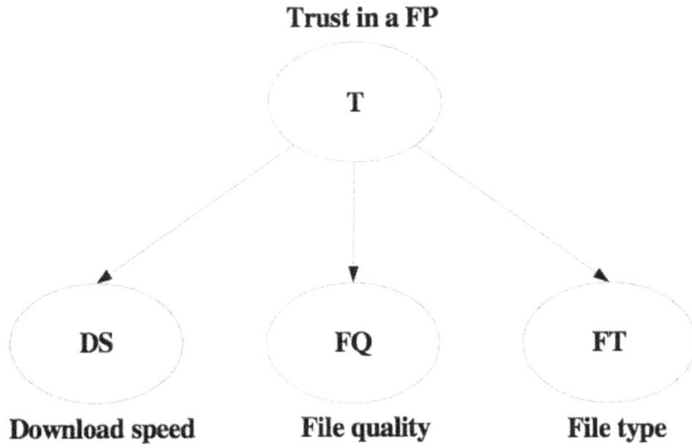

Fig. 3.4 A simple Bayesian network model of trust based on aspects of performance, taken from [106]. The model shows trust being computed in a File Provider (FP).

the node considers download speed, file quality, and file type when deciding whether or not to trust another node. If a node does not have the necessary information, it can ask other peers for recommendations. Those recommendations are aggregated with a weighted average, where those weights come from a comparison of peers' Bayesian networks.

One problem that is common to all of these algorithms, and those that will be discussed in Section 4, is how to treat new users. When a peer joins the system, it has no history and no connections. By default, new users are generally given a low level of trust, which makes it difficult for them to interact in the system and develop trust. Some systems present mechanisms to try to handle this; for example, in [78], the P2P system borrows relationships from existing social networks to create an initial set of trusted relationships for a node. However, in general the bootstrapping problem is a challenge for systems that use trust based on history.

3.3 Trust in Web-Services

The public first learned of the Semantic Web through an article in Scientific American by Tim Berners-Lee et al. in [15]. There, they presented a vision of devices, applications, and services working together seamlessly in a web-based environment. In particular, the agents, people, and services they describe have *trust* in one another:

> "The agent promptly retrieved information about Mom's prescribed treatment from the doctor's agent, looked up several lists of providers, and checked for the ones in-plan for Mom's insurance within a 20-mile radius of her home and with a rating of excellent or very good on **trusted** rating service."

and

> "Lucy's agent, having complete **trust** in Pete's agent in the context of the present task, automatically assisted by supplying access certificates and shortcuts to the data it had already sorted through." (emphasis added).

The trust described here is different than the quality of service-based trust of P2P systems. While trust is still used to control interactions between services, web service trust regulates the service requester's access to the service provider. Some of this is done through secure authentication schemes. This builds user trust in the web service because access and identities are protected. Beyond authentication, web services can build trust in more complex ways through policies that specify requirements for access. The research that has risen up around trust in web services captures this, with work on policy specification, trust negotiation, and evaluation. Web service policy is a broad space, and in this section, we will restrict our coverage to an overview of the efforts and core concepts in using policies for trust in web services.

On the web, describing policies requires a language. There are many proposals for ontology languages to specify policies, including [72], [25], [48], and XACML [75] to name just a few. Web Service Policy (WS-Policy [103]) is the current standards effort toward developing a a framework for representing web service policies. Both XACML and WS-Policy are XML-based languages, and recent work has provided a formal semantics for them using OWL-DL [67], [66]. This allows for existing Semantic Web tools to be used for evaluating policies, and improving trust.

Within WS-Policy, a *policy assertion* represents a behavioral requirement or property, such as quality of service or transport protocol. Policy assertions are collected into *policy alternatives*. A policy is a group of policy alternatives. These policies can specify authentication schemes, transport protocol, privacy policies, or quality of service characteristics among other things. These build trust in both directions. Users will be more likely to trust the services because of these features, and the services know they are interacting with trusted authenticated individuals.

The Web Services Trust Language (WS-Trust) [1] is built to create and broker trust relationships between parties by issuing and verifying tokens. These tokens reflect one service's credentials to access another service. The foundations for issuing a token can be based on a policy or other security qualifications. Trust can be established directly between services, or brokered when necessary. In a brokered trust relationship, an intermediate third party can vouch for one party to another.

To satisfy a policy, services must often exchange credentials — assertions that describe the service's attributes. This exchange takes place so the requester can prove that it satisfies the provider's requirements. Since some credentials are sensitive, a requester may require credentials from the provider, to prove that it should share the sensitive information. This exchange is a trust negotiation, and it requires frameworks, strategies, and models to be implemented.

There are several frameworks for negotiating trust. The TrustBuilder framework [108] describes strategies and protocols for negotiation, including which credentials to disclose and how to end negotiations. The Trust-Serv framework [98] provides a higher level of support. They use a state machine model for representing trust negotiations, upon which different strategies can be deployed. PeerTrust [85] is another framework for trust negotiation on the Semantic web. It uses guarded distributed logic programs to express and negotiate trust on the web. Digital credentials are used to prove access rights, and the negotiation process helps protect sensitive credentials from falling into the wrong hands.

Once policies have been specified, and credentials exchanged, trust management systems determine if a requested action conforms to the provider's policies given the requester's credentials. Most of the frameworks mentioned above include policy evaluation mechanisms, and the work in [66] allows OWL reasoners to be used for evaluating WS-Policy and XACML policies.

3.4 Conclusions

In this section, we have looked at how trust applies to services on the web, particularly in P2P systems and web services. In P2P, trust is generally determined by the attributes of peers — performance, price, speed, etc. The challenges to using trust is in managing and propagating that information through the network. We have seen several frameworks and algorithms that support this. For web services, some similar issues apply. Research in this space has gone a step beyond the techniques used in P2P, to involve complex access control policies and negotiations, which protect the information sent by both parties.

4

Trust in People

We have seen that "trust" is used in a variety of ways in computing literature. Social trust is emerging as an important computational problem. In open and distributed systems, like the web, people and organizations can be anonymous. Applications also bring together information from a variety of distributed sources, often in ways hidden from the user. Deciding who and what information to trust can be difficult in environments where the user does not have any direct knowledge of them. The dramatic proliferation of social networks and participation in online communities has created a data source from which trust relationships can be studied, computed, linked to data, and integrated into interfaces. Thus, the need for social trust and the ability to compute it have co-evolved.

Social Networking is one of the largest movements on the web, with hundreds of millions of user accounts among hundreds of different networks. Within those networks, users can express trust in other users in a variety of ways. Because this data is on the web and, therefore, public, the networks and trust relationships can be harnessed. The social networks where this trust is stored serve as trust management systems for trust in people; they maintain the trust values and provide a point of interaction where those values can be accessed and aggregated. In this section, we will see an overview of trust in web-based social networks and look at the different algorithms for computing trust relationships between individuals with no direct connection.

4.1 Web-Based Social Networks

Web-based social networks (WBSN) have grown quickly in number and scope since the mid-1990s. They present an interesting challenge to traditional ways of thinking about social networks. First, they are large, living examples of social networks. It has rarely, if ever, been possible to look at an actual network of millions of people without using models to fill in or simulate most of the network. The problem of gathering social information about a large group of people has been a difficult one. With WBSNs, there are many networks with millions of users that need no generated data. These networks are also much more complex with respect to the types of relationships they allow. Information qualifying and quantifying aspects of the social connection between people is common in these systems. This means there is a potential for much richer analysis of the network.

There are about 250 websites dedicated to social networking, i.e. they have explicit support for users to build and browse lists of friends. This includes websites like MySpace, Facebook, Orkut, and CyWorld but does not include many dating sites, like Match.com, and other online communities that connect users, such as Craig's List or MeetUp.com. The latter group of sites also contain social network information, but we do not consider them to be "Web-based Social Networks."

WBSNs have many purposes. We group them into the following general categories:

- Blogging
- Business
- Dating
- Pets
- Photos
- Religious
- Social/Entertainment

A list of all social networks we know of is maintained at http:// trust.mindswap.org/. There is incredible diversity among the sites in all dimensions. They range from having hundreds of millions of users to only a few dozen. They also have a range of expressivity about relationships between people. Some limit social connections to a basic friendship relationship while others provide many relationship types and options to carefully describe how people know each other.

4.1.1 Growth of Social Networks

There has been dramatic growth in the number and size of these networks. The number of sites almost doubled over the two year period from December 2004 to December 2006, growing from 125 to 223. Over the same period, the total number of members among all sites grew fourfold from 115 million to 490 million [42].

The size of individual networks ranges widely from a few dozen members to over 200 million members. In late 2006, the largest site (MySpace with more than 150 million members at the time) is nearly an order of magnitude larger than the largest site in 2004 (Tickle with 18 million members). As would be expected with this kind of growth, the number of WBSNs with over a million members has increased sharply from 18 in late 2004 to 41 in late 2006. While the number of sites has doubled and the total membership has increased many-fold, the *pattern* of distribution of members, as shown in Figure 4.1, is basically the same.

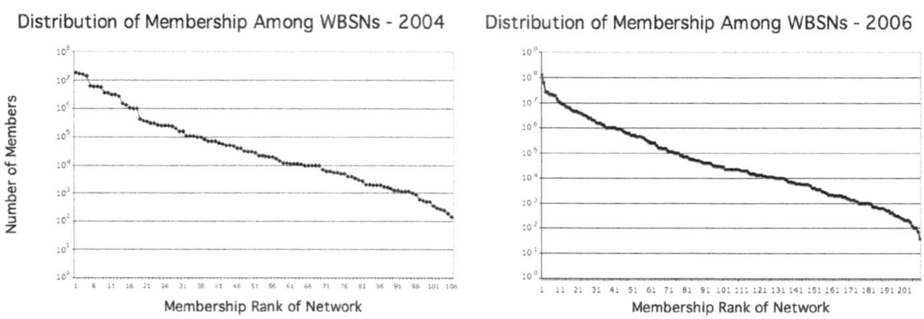

Fig. 4.1 Distribution of members among social networking websites in 2004. Sites are ranked from the most populated to least. Note that the y-axis is a logarithmic scale.

4.1.2 FOAF: Social Networks on the Semantic Web

Many people maintain accounts at multiple social networking websites. It is desirable, for example, to keep information intended for business networking separate from information about dating. People's bosses or colleagues certainly do not need to know that they enjoy long walks on the beach. At the same time, users put significant effort into maintaining information on social networks. Multiple social network accounts are not just for compartmentalizing parts of their lives. A person may have one group of friends who prefer MySpace, another group on Facebook, like the quiz features of Tickle, and have an account on one or two religious websites to stay connected to that community.

At the same time, from the perspective of managing an entire set of social connections that are spread across sites, it is advantageous to merge all of those connections together into one set of data. In a merged social network, friends who have multiple accounts would be represented as a single person. Information about the user that is distributed across several sites also would be merged. The Friend-of-a-Friend (FOAF) Project [33] is a potential solution to sharing social networking data among sites, and this section introduces how that is being done.

Rather than a website or a software package, FOAF is a framework for representing information about people and their social connections. The FOAF Vocabulary [19] contains terms for describing personal information, membership in groups, and social connections. The property "knows" is used to create social links between people (i.e., one person knows another person).

Using the basic features of RDF and OWL, it is easy to indicate that information about a person is contained in several documents on the web and provide links to those documents. Any tool that understands these languages will be able to take information from these distributed sources and create a single model of that person, merging the properties from the disparate sites.

If a website builds FOAF profiles of its users, it allows the users to own their data in a new way. Instead of having their information locked in a proprietary database, they are able to share it and link it.

Some WBSNs are already moving in this direction. At current count, 21 web-based social networks are creating FOAF files for over 15,000,000 users.

With this information, a user with accounts on all of these sites can create a small document that points to the generated files. An FOAF tool would follow those links and compile all of the information into a single profile. Aside from the benefit to users who are able to merge their data, websites are also able to benefit from FOAF data on the web. For example, a website could suggest connections to other users in their system if FOAF data from another site shows a connection between the two people. Some user information could be pre-filled in if it is contained in an FOAF file somewhere else. By enhancing the user experience, a site becomes easier and more attractive to use.

FOAF is being extended by other groups to add complexity to the way people can describe their relationships. There is a Trust Module for FOAF [47] that allows people to rate how much they trust one another on a scale from 1 to 10. Trust can be assigned in general or with respect to a particular topic. There is also FOAF Relationship Module [30] with over 30 terms for describing the relationships between people, including "lost contact with," "enemy of," "employed by," "spouse of," and others along those lines. A WBSN could co-opt these terms, or define its own set of relationship terms or personal characteristics to include in the FOAF data about its users.

4.2 Computing Trust in Social Networks

When two individuals know each other, they know how much to trust one another. Two people who are not directly connected do not have a foundation for knowing about trust. However, the paths connecting them in the network contain information that can be used to infer how much they may trust one another.

For example, consider that Alice trusts Bob, and Bob trusts Charlie. Although Alice does not know Charlie, she knows and trusts Bob who, in turn, has information about how trustworthy he believes Charlie is. Alice can use information from Bob and her own trust in Bob to infer how much she may trust Charlie. This is illustrated in Figure 4.2.

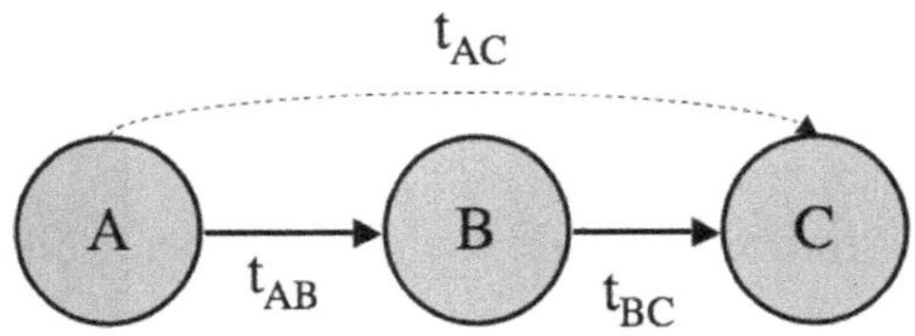

Fig. 4.2 An illustration of direct trust values between nodes A and B (t_{AB}), and between nodes B and C (t_{BC}). Using a trust inference algorithm, it is possible to compute a value to recommend how much A may trust C (t_{AC}).

Many of the algorithms for computing trust in P2P networks can be directly applied to social networks. However, there are also some unique features of social networks that require different algorithmic features.

There are several algorithms that infer trust relationships by utilizing the trust values along paths connecting the source and sink. They output a recommendation to the source about how much to trust the sink. In this section, we present several of the most prominent trust inference algorithms. It is difficult to compare the performance of these algorithms, because they are designed for different purposes.

4.2.1 Properties of Trust

Even though the algorithms presented in this section function in many different ways, there are properties of trust that they rely on. In this section, we discuss the functional properties of trust that play a role in inference methods.

4.2.1.1 Composability and Transitivity

The primary property of trust used in many of the algorithms is a limited kind of transitivity. Trust is not perfectly transitive in the mathematical sense; that is, if Alice highly trusts Bob, and Bob highly trusts Chuck, it does not always and exactly follow that Alice will highly trust Chuck. There is, however, a notion that trust can be passed between people. When we ask a trusted friend for an opinion about a plumber, we are taking the friend's opinion and incorporating that to help form a preliminary opinion of the plumber. Generally, when encountering an unknown person, it is common for people to ask trusted friends for opinions about how much to trust this new person. Computationally, this idea of propagating trust along chains of connections (thus exploiting some form of transitivity) has been widely studied and implemented [39, 49, 50, 57, 81, 116].

Transitivity describes how a trust rating can be passed back through a chain of people, but trust from multiple sources must also be composed together in all of these algorithms. Exactly how to compose trust is handled differently in each algorithm, but the fact that it *can* be composed is essential to all of them.

4.2.1.2 Personalization, Symmetry, and Context

Another important consideration with trust is the context. A person may trust someone to recommend a restaurant, but not to fix a car. The algorithms discussed below all impose a context on the trust values used. Similarly, the P2P trust inference algorithms discussed in Section 3.2 have a very specific P2P context for judging trust.

Another property of trust that is important in social networks is the personalization of trust. Trust is inherently a personal opinion. Two people often have very different opinions about the trustworthiness of the same person. For example, we need only look to politics. In the United States, the population will be split when asked, "do you trust the current President to effectively lead the country?" Some will trust him very highly, and the others will have very little trust in his abilities.

When trust is personalized, the asymmetry of trust is also important, and it reflects a specific type of personalization. For two people involved in a relationship, trust is not necessarily identical in both directions. Because individuals have different experiences, psychological backgrounds, and histories, it is understandable why two people may trust each other different amounts. For example, parents and children clearly trust one another at different levels, since the children are not capable of many tasks. This strong asymmetry can occur in other relationships where the people involved are on close social levels. This can be carried out fully to "one-way trust" where circumstances force one person to trust the other, but there is no reciprocal trust [26, 53]. However, most asymmetry is not as extreme as any of those circumstances. Most trust is mutual [53] in that each party has some trust for the other, but there are still often differences in how much they trust one another. For example, employees typically say they trust their supervisors more than the supervisors trust the employees. This is seen in a variety of hierarchies [110]. Asymmetric trust can arise in any relationship, and representations of trust relationships in models of social networks must allow for these differences.

One of the major distinguishing characteristics of a trust inference algorithm is whether it considers personalization, and is a *local trust algorithm*, or if it computes a single trust value for each user, and is a *global trust algorithm*. The global approach is appropriate in applications where trust reflects behavior that is universally considered good or bad. For example, if trust is used to permit or deny rights to publish content within a collaborative website, a global trust algorithm would be appropriate since basically all users agree on general notions of good and bad contents (e.g., spam). In other contexts, a local metric may be more appropriate. Local trust inference algorithms compute different values for the sink based on who the source is. When the application is one that is opinion-based, and there is no shared idea of good and bad or right and wrong, a local trust metric should be used to compute a rating that most closely matches the preferences of the source.

4.2.2 Trust Inference Algorithms

Advogato is a website, at http://advogato.org, that serves as a community discussion board and resource for free software developers. It also is the testbed for Raph Levien's trust metrics research [73]. Each user on the site has a single trust rating calculated from the perspective of designated seeds (authoritative nodes). Trust calculations are made using the maximum trust flow along a path from one of the authoritative seeds to the user. His metric composes certifications between members to determine the trust level of a person, and thus their membership within a group. Users can be certified at three levels: apprentice, journeyer, and master. Access to post and edit website information is controlled by these certifications. Like EigenTrust, the Advogato metric is quite attack resistant. By identifying individual nodes as "bad" and finding any nodes that certify the "bad" nodes, the metric cuts out an unreliable portion of the network. Calculations are based primarily on the good nodes, so the network as a whole remains secure. It is a global trust algorithm because the same seeds are used to make calculations for every user. Advogato is also a group trust metric because it uses groups to determine who can post messages. A common alteration to Advogato sets the user as the single seed, thus converting it to a local metric with personalized calculations.

Matthew et al. [81] use social networks with trust to calculate the belief a user may have in a statement. This is done by finding paths (either through enumeration or probabilistic methods) from the source to any node which represents an opinion of the statement in question, concatenating trust values along the paths to come up with the recommended belief in the statement for that path, and aggregating those values to come up with a final trust value for the statement. Their paper intentionally does not define a specific concatenation function for calculating trust between individuals, opting instead to present a general framework as their main result. To test their algorithms, they do choose a concatenation function (multiplication) and demonstrate the accuracy of their results using the Epinions network.

TidalTrust [39] is a trust algorithm that also uses trust values within the social network. It is a modified breadth-first search. The source's inferred trust rating for the sink ($t_{\text{source, sink}}$) is a weighted average if the source's neighbors' ratings of the sink. The source node begins a search for the sink. It will poll each of its neighbors to obtain their rating of the sink. If the neighbor has a direct rating of the sink, that value is returned. If the neighbor does not have a direct rating for the sink, it queries all of its neighbors for their ratings, computes the weighted average, and returns the result. Each neighbor repeats this process. Essentially, the nodes perform a breadth-first search from the source to the sink. In this algorithm, nodes keep a running record of the search depth and the minimum trust value along each path. These are available to limit the information that is considered so that the result is as accurate as possible. TidalTrust was evaluated in two social networks and shown to predict trust values that were within approximately 10% of the known values.

MoleTrust [79] works in two steps. The first builds a directed acyclic graph from the source to all nodes within a fixed distance, known as the *Trust Propagation Horizon*. Cycles are removed by deleting edges from a node to another node that is equidistant or closer to the source. The second step uses this DAG to compute trust in the sink. MoleTrust first computes the trust score of all the users within one step of the sink, then of all the users within two steps, and so on. Once the trust values for the intermediate nodes are computed, they are used to compute the trust in the sink. That value is given by the average of the incoming trust values to the sink, weighted by the computed trust in the nodes that assigned those trust values. To improve accuracy, the algorithm ignores any information from nodes whose trust value is less than 0.6 on a 0–1 scale. Note that it is only possible to compute trust in the sink if it is within the trust propagation horizon of the source.

Ziegler and Lausen [116] propose a trust algorithm called Appleseed. Like Advogato, it is a group trust metric. However, instead of using maximum flow, it employs spreading activation strategies to produce a trust ranking of individuals in the network. They modify traditional spreading activation models to account for trust decay. Consider Figure 4.3. Without trust decay, the trust rank node a computes for

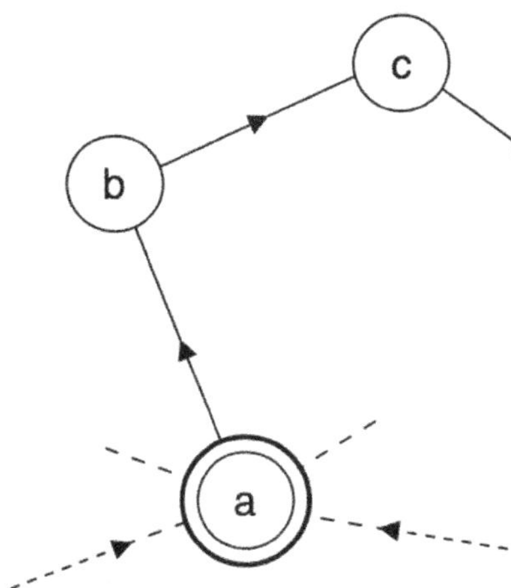

Fig. 4.3 A small sample social network. With no trust decay in the Appleseed algorithm, a would compute equal trust ranks for b and d.

node b will be the same as the trust rank for node d. However, as paths grow longer, we would expect the trust to decrease to account for uncertainty. This is decay is built into algorithms like TidalTrust and MoleTrust, and is made explicit in Appleseed. The algorithm also handles cycles, normalization of trust values, and backward propagation. When it is run, Appleseed is run repeatedly. At each step the trust rank of a node is updated, and because social networks contain cycles, the rank will converge. The algorithm terminates when the difference in rank between step $t-1$ and t is within a specified threshold.

If trust is used to support decision making, it is important to have an accurate estimate of trust when it is not directly available, as well as a measure of confidence in that estimate. The algorithms described above address confidence within their trust estimates by limiting the depth of searches or applying thresholds on trust. The SUNNY algorithm [70] computes trust with an explicit probabilistic interpretation for confidence in social networks. Confidence can be derived from explicit user statements or by using other data available in the system that hosts the social network. SUNNY uses a probabilistic sampling technique to estimate confidence in the trust information provided by some designated sources. SUNNY computes an estimate of trust based on only those information sources with high confidence estimates, and outputs both the computed trust value and a confidence estimate in that value.

Guha et al. [50] present a method for propagating both trust and *distrust* through social networks. Propagating distrust is a difficult issue. Consider Figure 4.2, and let the edges represent distrust relationships. If A distrusts B, and B distrusts C, what opinion can A form about C? Should A trust C, following the idea that "the enemy of my enemy is my friend," or should A distrust C even more than B, because "if someone I distrust as much as B can't even trust C, I certainly should not." Guha et al. [50] presents these options as multiplicative and additive distrust propagation, respectively. The problem in choosing a method is that it requires an understanding of the context and the user's intent. For these reasons, the authors in [50] do not commit to a particular type of propagation. Instead, they conduct a series of experiments using Epinions with a variety of trust and distrust propagation methods. They also focus on techniques for rounding the final values to make them discrete, as is often how they are assigned in the systems. The authors conclude that the combination of techniques most appropriate will vary depending on the application and context.

Distrust propagation is handled in another local trust method based on subjective logic called TNA-SL [58]. To propagate distrust, all of the intermediate nodes along a path must have positive trust; this avoids the problem of a chain of distrust that must be interpreted.

Given the difficulty of crafting algorithms that deal with distrust as a separate dimension while respecting intuition, and given the fact that no one so far has presented a compelling case that evaluation of distrust has a separate role to play from that of evaluation of trust, we would have to argue that understanding distrust should not be a central topic of research in this field.

4.3 Conclusions

The web has always been a place where people interact with information and increasingly it is a place where people interact with one another. Social networking has become an important movement on the web in general, and on the Semantic Web, via FOAF, in particular. For human interactions, trust will always be an important relationship, and that is reflected in the research about trust between people on the web.

In this section, we have looked at the properties and dynamics of web-based social networks, and algorithms for computing trust in those networks. Unlike trust in P2P and web service networks, the application that uses the trust values is not paired directly with social networks. In the next section, we explore some applications that are independent of but utilize trust from social networks.

5

Applications

So far, we have looked at trust in services, people, and content. When trust is established, the natural next step is to create applications that take advantage of those values. In this section, we look at a range of applications that utilize trust, including recommender systems and email filters.

5.1 Recommender Systems

Recommender systems help users identify items of interest. These recommendations are generally made in two ways: by calculating the similarity between items and recommending items related to those in which the user has expressed interest, or by calculating the similarity between users in the system and recommending items that are liked by similar users. This latter method is also known as collaborative filtering.

Collaborative filtering (which does not rely on social networks) has been applied in many contexts, MovieLens [54], Recommendz [37], and Film-Conseil [89] are just a few examples. Herlocker et al. [55] present an excellent overview of the goals, datasets, and algorithms of collaborative filtering systems. There are several challenges to these systems.

Since collaborative filtering relies on computing similarity measures between users, new users pose a problem because they do not have any items rated that would allow similarity to be computed. Second, even for users with many ratings, the datasets are often sparse such that pairs of users have very few items in common. An alternative to traditional collaborative filtering is to use trust in place of similarity.

For this technique to be successful, there must be a correlation between trust and user similarity. Abdul-Rahman and Hailes [2] showed that in a predefined context, such as movies, users develop social connections with people who have similar preferences.

These results were extended in work by Ziegler and Lausen [115] that showed a correlation between trust and user similarity in an empirical study of a real online community. Using All Consuming,[1] an online community where users rate books. The authors showed that users were significantly more similar to their trusted peers than to the population as a whole. This work was extended in [114] to include an analysis of the All Consuming community and added an analysis. The second result in [114] used the FilmTrust system [40] (described below) where users have stated how much they trust their friends in a social network and also rated movies. Within that community, results also showed a strong correlation between trust and similarity in movie ratings.

Beyond general similarity, [41] presents a controlled study to identify nuanced similarity measures that reflect trust. Consider the case where two users rate the same 10 movies. This includes the favorite and least favorite movies of the first user. If the second user hates the favorite movie and loves the least favorite movie, but agrees perfectly on the other 8 films, overall similarity will be high. However, if the second user agrees perfectly on the favorite and least favorite movie, but has some differences on the other 8, similarity will be lower, but trust may not be lower. Intuitively, agreement on movies that are important to the first user will have a bigger impact on trust. The study in [41] identified three similarity measures that significantly impact trust: overall similarity (confirming the results in [115] and [114]), similarity on items with ratings on the extreme ends of the scale (as in the example given here),

[1] http://allconsuming.net/.

and the single largest difference between users. The results also showed that individuals' propensity to trust varies greatly from one person to the next, and that also significantly impacts trust ratings they assign. These survey results were composed into a formula for estimating trust based on rating similarities, and verified within the FilmTrust system.

Furthermore, there is evidence to support that users will prefer systems with recommendations that rely on social networks and trust relationships over similarity measures commonly used for making recommendations. Research has shown that people prefer recommendations from friends to those made by recommender systems [97] and that users prefer recommendations from systems they trust [101]. By producing recommendations through the use of trust in social networks, both of those user preferences are addressed. Recommendations come through a network of friends, and are based on the explicit trust expressed by the user. While this is certainly not the same as having recommendations come directly from friends, social trust-based recommendations reflect a more nuanced type of similarity than is used by traditional recommender systems [41], and thus they may come closer to capturing some of the benefits that users find in recommendations from friends.

Empirical results show that trust can improve recommendations. Some of those results are described in the particular applications below. O'Donovan and Smyth [86] performed an analysis of how trust impacts the accuracy of recommendations in recommender systems. Using the MovieLens dataset [83], they create trust-values by estimating how accurately a person predicted the preferences of another. Those trust values were then used in connection with a traditional collaborative filtering algorithm [68], and an evaluation showed significant improvement in the accuracy of the recommendations.

Massa and Bhattacharjee [80] also conducted a study on the applicability of trust in recommender systems. Their study relied on the user ratings of products and trust ratings of other users from epinions[2] as their dataset. Using a trust propagation algorithm, similar to those described in Section 4.2, they showed that trust based

[2] http://epinions.com.

recommendations could perform significantly better than those based on similarity alone.

With this background as motivation, there have been several applications developed to utilize social trust to create predictive recommendations.

5.1.1 FilmTrust

FilmTrust [40], at http://trust.mindswap.org/FilmTrust, is a website that uses trust to make movie recommendations. Within the site, users can rate movies and write reviews. They also maintain friends lists, as is typical of social networking websites, and they also assign trust ratings to indicate how much they trust their friends about movies.

This information is combined on the movie information pages in the system (see Figure 5.1). Users are shown two ratings for each movie.

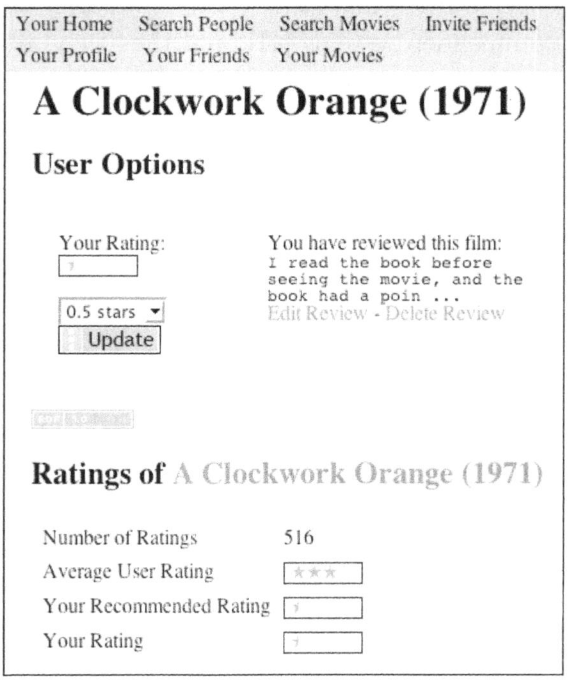

Fig. 5.1 A sample of a recommended rating in the FilmTrust system.

The first is the simple average of all ratings given to the film. The "Recommended Rating" is a weighted average of the movie ratings where the weights are given by the user's trust in each person who rated the film.

The "Recommended Rating" is personalized using the trust values for the people who have rated the film (the raters). First, the system searches for raters that the source knows directly. If there are no direct connections from the user to any raters, the system moves one step out to find connections from the user to raters of path length 2. This process repeats until a path is found. The opinion of all raters at that depth are considered. Then, using a trust inference algorithm, the trust value is calculated for each rater at the given depth. Once every rater has been given an trust value, only raters trusted above a specified threshold will be selected. Finally, once the raters have been selected, their ratings for the movie (in number of stars) are averaged, with trust values used as a weight. This average is rounded to the nearest half-star, and that value becomes the "Recommended Rating" that is personalized for each user.

The accuracy of this approach was judged by comparing the trust-based recommendation with the user's known rating of a movie. Error was measured as the absolute difference. This was compared to the error using the simple average rating of a movie as the recommendation, and the predictive rating generated by a simple correlation-based automated collaborative filtering algorithm. Results are shown in Figure 5.2.

For all users and all movies, the three techniques perform statistically identically. However, intuition suggests that trust-based recommendations will be most effective when the user is different from the general population.

Results showed that when the user's rating of a movie is different than the average rating, it is likely that the recommended rating will more closely reflect the user's tastes. As the magnitude of this difference increases, the benefit offered by the trust-based recommendation also increases. Based on these findings, the recommended ratings should be useful when people have never seen a movie.

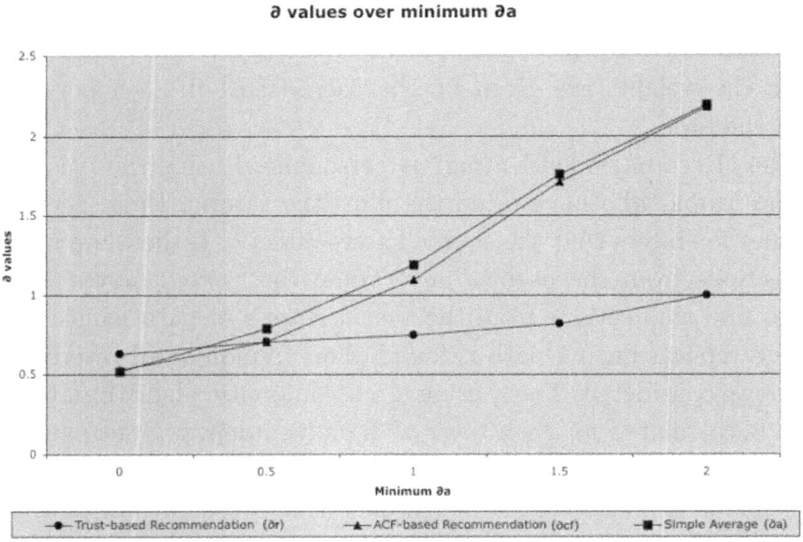

Fig. 5.2 Accuracy of predicted ratings in the FilmTrust system. The y-axis is a measure of error, and these results show error increases more slowly for the trust-based ratings as the user's opinion grows different from the average.

5.1.2 Moleskiing

Moleskiing [11], at http://moleskiing.it, is another real system built to utilize trust ratings in a recommender system. The subject of the website is ski mountaineering. Their goal is to make the activity safer by collecting information from users about the conditions and quality of ski trails. Users also express how much they trust one another, and those ratings are used to personalize the recommendations.

Moleskiing separates information into ski routes, which are relatively static and entered by experts, and ski trips, which are dynamic comments entered by users. Ski trip information is maintained on Moleskiing-hosted blogs. In addition to keeping blogs on the site, users have lists of their friends and how much they trust them. Then, using a trust metric to compute trust values for unknown users, the system recommends routes, which are ranked by their average rating, weighted by the user's trust in the creator of the recommendation.

Because ski conditions change, Moleskiing also uses temporal filters, favoring information created within two weeks of the time users interact with the system. For example, the homepage (shown in Figure 5.3), shows only routes rated as secure in the last 15 days by the majority of trustable users.

An interesting feature of Moleskiing is that it does not require the system to be centralized. It is built to rely on Semantic Web data. FOAF is used to model the social network, and an ontology is also used to represent the trust values in the system.

5.2 News Syndication

The interest in web-based syndication systems has been growing, as information streams onto the web at an increasing rate. Millions of people are using RSS feeds to subscribe to information published online.

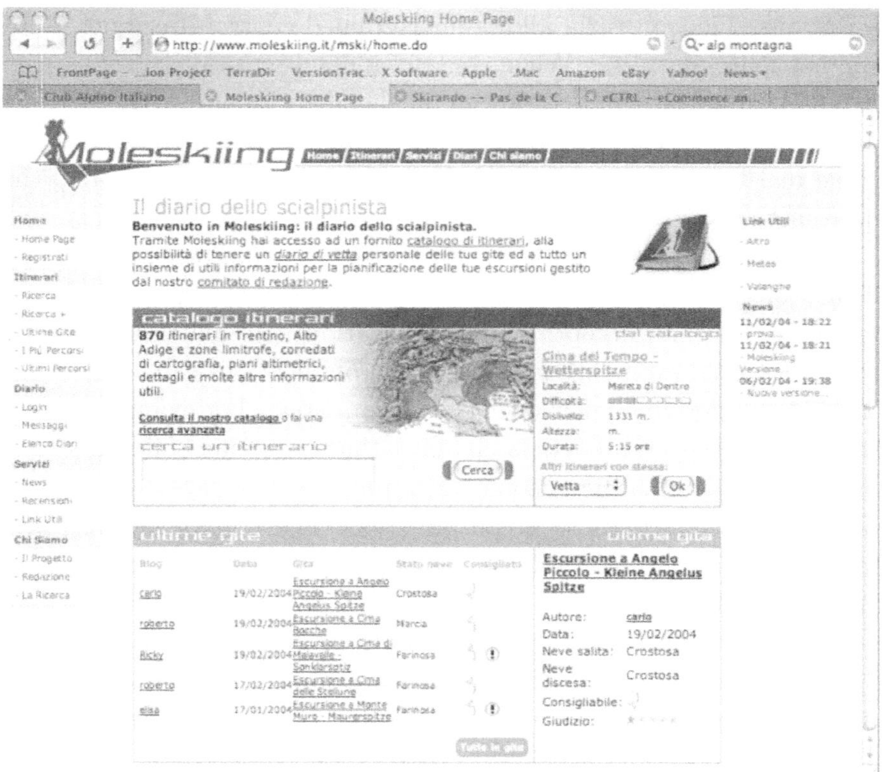

Fig. 5.3 A screenshot of the Moleskiing homepage.

As the amount of content published to the web and interest in it has increased, technologies for sharing information in a machine processable way have matured on the web. This has increased the power available to publishers to describe their content, to consumers to describe their subscriptions, and to brokers for matching content to subscriptions. There has been a transition from keyword based approaches [87] to attribute-value pairs (e.g., [7]) and more recently to XML [8, 31]. Given the limited knowledge modeling expressivity of XML (and XML Schema) there has been interest in using RDF for syndication purposes [24, 105]. RDF has even been adopted as the standard representation format of RSS 1.0.[3]

Halaschek-Wiener [52] develops techniques to support using Semantic Web technologies for syndication. Using OWL for describing web content offers much greater expressivity for describing content and subscriptions. That, in turn, allows finer grained control over queries and content matching [102]. When content and subscriptions are described in OWL, the matching task can be handled using OWL reasoners [51, 74, 102]. When the content can be processed and reasoned over, these real time news feeds can help activities, like stock trading, that need fast access to information.

The challenges to such a system is based on the computational difficulty of OWL reasoning. The work in [52] creates optimizations to reasoning tasks for accepting new publications and matching subscriptions. However, even with fast reasoning, publications can come in that make the underlying knowledge base inconsistent. For example, if news source X publishes an article claiming that a specific children's toy is dangerous, and then news source Y publishes an article claiming that same toy is safe, there is a contradiction. The knowledge base must remain free of contradictions, so one of these stories must be discarded. Which one should it be?

One of the approaches described in [52] and [43] uses trust to choose. Specifically, if the broker receives a publication that causes a contradiction, the statements from the least trusted sources will be discarded. This is formalized as a belief-based revision approach for knowledge

[3] RSS 1.0 Specification: http://web.resource.org/rss/1.0/spec.

bases. When a publication is received that causes the knowledge base to become inconsistent, the algorithm finds sets of statements that lead to the contradiction. Each set is called a kernel. By removing one statement from each kernel, the knowledge base is guaranteed to regain consistency. An *incision function* is used to select the statements to remove from each kernel. The authors define a trust-based incision function. Using provenance techniques similar to those described in 2.4, the source of each statement in a kernel is identified. Then, the trust that the user has in each source is found, either by direct lookup or by using a trust inference algorithm (such as those presented in 4.2). The statement made by the least trusted source is selected to be removed. This regains consistency in the knowledge base and keeps the most trusted information. The research includes general descriptions of how trust can be balanced with other important factors, such as how recently each article was published.

5.3 Email Filtering

The fact that spam has become such a ubiquitous problem with email has lead to much research and development of algorithms that try to identify spam and prevent it from even reaching the user's mailbox. Many of those techniques have been highly successful, catching, and filtering a majority of spam messages that a person receives.

Though work still continues to refine these methods, some focus has shifted to new mechanisms for blocking unwanted messages and highlighting good, or valid, messages. Whitelist filters are one of these methods. In these systems, users create a list of approved addresses from which they will accept messages. Any whitelisted messages are delivered to the user's inbox, and all others are filtered into a low-priority folder. Blacklist filters, where users create a list of blocked email addresses, are generally less comprehensive but serve the same purpose of cutting back on unwanted mail.

Though whitelists are nearly 100% effective at blocking unwanted email, there are two major problems cited with them. First, there is an extra burden placed on the user to maintain a whitelist, and second, valid emails will almost certainly be filtered into the low-priority mailbox. If that box contains a lot of spam, the valid messages will be especially difficult to find.

Social filtering is an interesting space of research in combating spam; the premise behind it is that users can trust messages from people they know more than messages from unknown people. Many of these methods preserve the whitelist benefit of making the inbox more usable by making "good" messages prominent, while also blocking bad messages. In this section, we will look at research into methods for social and trust-based email filtering, as well as work that addresses the applicability of such approaches.

5.3.1 Filtering Techniques

Since the early days of the web, there has been work on filtering email using social techniques. One of the first projects in this space was Maxims [71], an agent integrated with an email client that learns how to filter, delete, and archive messages based on user actions. When a given user's agent does not have knowledge about how to handle a situation, it can look to other user's agents for help. Over time, agents develop "trust" in one another based on previous interactions. Their results show that using trust and collaboration, agents are able to effectively make suggestions regarding email filtering.

Since 1994, email filtering research has been dominated by the spam issue. New social filtering techniques seek to remove spam, but also offer other assistance to users in handling their message. Boykin and Roychowdhury [18] create a social network from the messages that a user has received. Using the structural properties of social networks, particularly the propensity for local clustering, messages are identified as spam, valid, or unknown based on clustering thresholds. Their method is able to classify about 50% of a user's email into the spam or valid categories, leaving 50% to be filtered by other techniques.

While Boykin and Roychowdhury's technique builds a social network from the user's own email folders, a broader outside social network can also be used for filtering email. Messages can be scored by the trust in the sender, computed using some of the techniques described in Section 4.

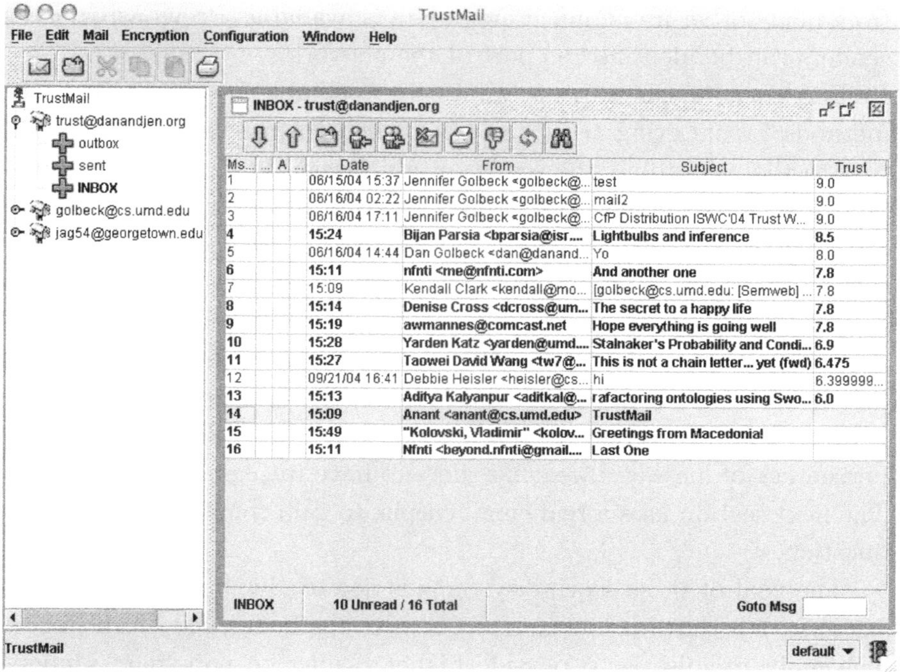

Fig. 5.4 A screenshot of the TrustMail interface.

TrustMail [44] is a prototype email client that adds trust ratings to the folder views of a message. (see Figure 5.4) This allows a user to see their trust rating for each individual, and sort messages accordingly. This is, essentially, a message scoring system. The benefit to users is that relevant and potentially important messages can be highlighted, even if the user does not know the sender. The determination of whether or not a message is significant is made using the user's own perspective on the trust network, and thus scores will be personalized to and under the control of each user.

Techniques that build social networks from messages that the user has sent or received can identify whether or not a message has come from someone in the network. However, because they are built only from the user's local mail folders, no information is available about people that the user has not previously seen. If the user's personal network is connected in to a larger social network with information from many other users, much more data is available. Previously unseen senders can be identified as part of the network.

Furthermore, since trust values are available in the system, the methods for inferring trust can be applied to present more information to the user about the sender of a message. In the FilmTrust system, it was shown that users benefited from having ratings sorted by the trust in the author. These results are the basis for sorting messages by the trust in the sender in TrustMail. However, unlike the FilmTrust where every review was authored by someone in the social network, people will undoubtedly receive many email messages from people who are not in their social network. To understand what benefit TrustMail might offer to users, it is important to understand what percentage of messages we can expect to have ratings for in TrustMail. The next section uses a real email corpus to gain some insight into this question.

The goal of these scoring systems is not to give low ratings to bad senders, thus showing low numbers next to spam messages in the inbox. The main premise is to provide higher ratings to non-spam senders, so users are able to identify messages of interest that they might not otherwise have recognized. This puts a lower burden on the user, since there is no need to rate all of the spam senders.

Because of this focus, these algorithms are not intended to be a solution to spam; rather, they are techniques for use in conjunction with a variety of other anti-spam mechanisms. There are some spam issues that particularly affect this algorithm. Because social and trust-based scoring is designed to identify good messages that make it past spam filters, it also does not address the case where a person has a virus sending messages from their account. Other spam-detection techniques will be required to flag these messages.

"Spoofing," where a spammer forges the "from" address in an email is related to this, and it is a major problem for social systems. In [94], the authors present a system for creating "Trusted Email Addresses." They present an authentication mechanism that uses past history as well as a challenge and response system. The results of this can be combined with some of the social approaches discussed above to create a secure and trustworthy email system.

5.3.2 Applicability

One question that arises when considering email filtering approaches is how many messages could be connected to trust information. If this information is available for only a small number of messages, the impact of these filtering techniques is limited. Of course, running a study on this is very difficult because people are often unwilling to share their email. However, we can look at some real email collections to get a general idea of how applicable these techniques are.

The Enron email dataset is a collection of the mail folders of 150 Enron employees, and it contains over 1.5 million messages, both sent and received. There are over 6,000 unique senders in the corpus, and over 28,000 unique recipients. These numbers are much greater than the number of users whose mailboxes have been collected because they represent everyone who has sent a message to the users, everyone who has been cc-ed on a message to the users, and everyone the users have emailed. The collection was made available by the Federal Energy Regulatory Commission in late 2003 in response to the legal investigation of the company.

A social network can be built based on email messages exchanged (i.e., adding an edge between two people who have emailed one another). While this network does not have trust values, and does not indicate if the trust-based email filtering would work, it does provide insight into how many messages could be evaluated with these techniques.

An analysis of the Enron network showed the following statistics:

- 37% of recipients had direct connections to people who sent them email in the social network; in other words, 37% of the time the recipient had emailed the sender of a received message.
- 55% of senders who were not directly connected to the recipient could be reached through paths in the social network.
- Thus, a total of 92% of all senders can be rated if trust values were present in the social network.

Of course, each technique would need to be evaluated on real data, but this email collection shows that we can at least expect the algorithms would be able to provide some insight into the vast majority of senders.

These numbers indicate that users in a community like Enron, social email filtering can provide information about a vast majority of the incoming messages. While the Enron corpus is a close community of users, it is reasonable to expect that, if users are properly supported in making trust ratings as part of their email client, a similarly high percentage of senders and messages would receive ratings.

5.4 Peer to Peer Routing

In Section 3.2, we looked at algorithms designed for computing trust in peer to peer (P2P) systems. Those algorithms are generally used to select trusted peers to work with. SPROUT [78], on the other hand, relies on social networks and *a priori* trust to improve P2P routing. One of the problems in P2P systems is that peers may fail to properly route requests. Malicious nodes may drop or misroute messages or masquerade as multiple nodes in the network. The key insight in SPOUT is to use peers controlled by friends in social networks, because those friends are more likely to properly route messages. Similarly, peers controlled by friends of friends are expected to be more reliable than strangers.

Trust between two nodes in the social network is modeled as a function of the distance between them. A node that is only one step away is trusted more than a node two steps away, which, in turn, is trusted more than a node three steps away and so on. This trust information is used to create the Social Path ROUTing (SPROUT) algorithm. SPROUT is built on top of the Chord routing algorithm [100] and adds additional links to friends who are online.

SPROUT was evaluated against Chord to determine what improvement the trusted social connections provide. Because SPROUT adds additional links, a third algorithm — "augmented Chord" — is used in the analysis. In Augmented Chord, nodes are given a set of random links equal to the number they would receive in SPROUT. The results

Table 5.1 Reliability of the SRPOUT algorithm vs. Chord (taken from [78]).

	Avg. Path Length	Avg. Reliability
Regular chord	5.343	0.3080
Augmented chord	4.532	0.3649
SPROUT	4.569	0.4661

of their analysis shows that SPROUT significantly outperforms both Chord and augmented Chord (see Table 5.1).

6

Discussion and Conclusions

This review has covered a variety of approaches to understanding trust on the web. The web includes interaction among a variety of entities — people, services, and content. We argue that trust is a critical component for interactions between all of these entities, and as the science of the web progresses, so too must the understanding of trust in a web environment.

When it comes to content on the web, trust has always been a critical component. The vision of the Semantic Web puts trust as one of the ultimate goals. We looked at this goal, and reviewed work on several ways to improve trust in content and in the creators of content. Following from that, we described provenance systems that track the history and interconnections among data to improve users' understanding, and ultimately their trust in it.

Beyond content, web services, including peer-to-peer systems, require an infrastructure for trust. While some of these services are free and open, providing non-sensitive content like music downloads or book pricing, others involve the exchange of funds or more sensitive information. In these latter cases, it is necessary to establish trust between both parties. For P2P systems, that frequently involves sharing information about the performance and history of a peer to prove it can be trusted in a transaction. For web services, the trust negotiations can be even more complex, with policies on both sides regulating the exchange of information. We considered current work on managing, computing, and exchanging trust, and on representing and evaluating access control policies.

Finally, we looked at one of the newer areas of interaction on the web: social networking and direct interaction between people. Judgments about trust are present in almost all human interactions, and it is also important in web-based social interactions. We reviewed the phenomenon of web-based social networking, and looked at all the major algorithms for computing trust between non-adjacent users in the network.

These methods of computing and understanding trust come together in applications. In some contexts, like provenance, P2P, and web services, the application was inextricably linked with the issues of trust management and computation we discussed. Other applications were relatively independent, relying on trust to provide additional functionality.

I argue that this step of taking trust information and integrating it with applications is the major direction that trust research on the web will take. This will not only be building systems like recommenders or email filters. Much larger systems, which pull together services, social trust, and content-based trust are on the horizon. Different facets will require and benefit from different types of trust. All of these applications will demand new methods for evaluation. Many of the algorithms and systems presented in this review have not been evaluated in simulation or in real systems. Part of this is because privacy prevents much real trust data from being shared, and part of it is that the focus of a lot of this work has so far been on the theoretical side rather than the implementation side. As trust becomes a critical component of more applications, new benchmarks and standards of evaluation will need to be created.

Ultimately, the trust foundation of the web will be reflective of our non-internet lives, where trust permeates every aspect of our interactions in one way or another. In [14] the authors acknowledged that web science is an eclectic discipline, and the trust component of it may be one of the most eclectic components of it. However, if the challenges are met, it can also be the component that brings the most significant results.

Acknowledgments

Thanks to my students and colleagues who provided insight, information, and lots of help to bring this review into being, including Mariya Filippova, Chris Halaschek-Weiner, Jim Hendler, Vladimir Kolovski, Raph Levien, Paolo Massa, and Cai Ziegler. The reviews of this article were incredibly helpful, and the reviewers have my sincere gratitude. Many thanks also to Wendy Hall and James Finlay for their comments and support.

The author was supported by several sources during the writing of this review, including the Intelligence Community Postdoctoral Research Fellowship Program, the National Science Foundation, and funders of MINDSWAP including Fujitsu Laboratories of America — College Park, Lockheed Martin Advanced Technology Laboratory, NTT Corp., Kevric Corp., SAIC, the National Geospatial-Intelligence Agency, DARPA, US Army Research Laboratory, NIST, and other DoD sources.

References

[1] "Web services trust language," February 2005.

[2] A. Abdul-Rahman and S. Hailes, "Supporting trust in virtual communities," in *Proceedings of the 33rd Hawaii International Conference on System Sciences*, 2000.

[3] A. Abdul-Rahman and S. Hailes, "A distributed trust model," in *NSPW '97: Proceedings of the 1997 Workshop on New Security Paradigms*, pp. 48–60, New York, NY, USA: ACM Press, 1997.

[4] F. Abel, M. Frank, N. Henze, D. Krause, D. Plappert, and P. Siehndel, "Groupme! — where semantic web meets web 2.0," in *Proceedings of the 6th International Semantic Web Conference*, 2007.

[5] K. Aberer, "P-grid: A self-organizing access structure for P2P information systems," in *CooplS '01: Proceedings of the 9th International Conference on Cooperative Information Systems*, pp. 179–194, London, UK: Springer-Verlag, 2001.

[6] K. Aberer and Z. Despotovic, "Managing trust in a peer-2-peer information system," in *CIKM '01: Proceedings of the Tenth International Conference on Information and Knowledge Management*, pp. 310–317, New York, NY, USA: ACM Press, 2001.

[7] M. K. Aguilera, R. E. Strom, D. C. Sturman, M. Astley, and T. D. Chandra, "Matching events in a content-based subscription system," in *Symposium on Principles of Distributed Computing*, 1999.

[8] M. Altinel and M. J. Franklin, "Efficient filtering of XML documents for selective dissemination of information," in *The VLDB Journal*, 2000.

[9] A. Ansper, A. Buldas, M. Roos, and J. Willemson, "Efficient long-term validation of digital signatures," in *PKC '01: Proceedings of the 4th International*

Workshop on Practice and Theory in Public Key Cryptography, pp. 402–415, London, UK: Springer-Verlag, 2001.

[10] L. Aroyo, N. Stash, Y. Wang, P. Gorgels, and L. Rutledge, "Chip demonstrator: Semantics-driven recommendations and museum tour generation," in *Proceedings of the 6th International Semantic Web Conference*, 2007.

[11] P. Avesani, P. Massa, and R. Tiella, "Moleskiing.it: A trust-aware recommender system for ski mountaineering," *International Journal for Infonomics*, 2005.

[12] F. Baader, D. Calvanese, D. L. McGuinness, D. Nardi, and P. F. Patel-Schneider, eds., *The Description Logic Handbook: Theory, Implementation, and Applications*, Cambridge University Press, 2003.

[13] K. S. Barber and J. Kim, "Belief revision process based on trust: Agents evaluating reputation of information sources," in *Proceedings of the Workshop on Deception, Fraud, and Trust in Agent Societies held During the Autonomous Agents Conference*, pp. 73–82, London, UK: Springer-Verlag, 2001.

[14] T. Berners-Lee, W. Hall, J. A. Hendler, K. O'Hara, N. Shadbolt, and D. J. Weitzner, "A framework for web science," *Foundations and Trends(R) in Web Science*, 2006.

[15] T. Berners-Lee, J. Hendler, and O. Lassila, "The semantic web," *Scientific American*, May 2001.

[16] M. Blaze, J. Feigenbaum, J. Ioannidis, and A. D. Keromytis, *The Role of Trust Management in Distributed Systems Security*, pp. 185–210. London, UK: Springer-Verlag, 1999.

[17] M. Blaze, J. Feigenbaum, and J. Lacy, "Decentralized trust management," in *SP '96: Proceedings of the 1996 IEEE Symposium on Security and Privacy*, p. 164, Washington, DC, USA: IEEE Computer Society, 1996.

[18] P. O. Boykin and V. Roychowdhury, "Personal email networks: An effective anti-spam tool," *IEEE Computer*, vol. 38, p. 61, 2004.

[19] D. Brickley and L. Miller, "Foaf vocabulary specification, namespace document," 2004.

[20] J. J. Carroll, C. Bizer, P. Hayes, and P. Stickler, "Named graphs, provenance and trust," in *WWW '05: Proceedings of the 14th International Conference on World Wide Web*, pp. 613–622, New York, NY, USA: ACM, 2005.

[21] J. J. Carroll, P. Hayes, C. Bizer, and P. Stickler, "Named graphs, provenance and trust," in *Proceedings of the First International Semantic Web Conference*, 2002.

[22] O. Celma, "Foafing the music: Bridging the semantic gap in music recommendation," in *Proceedings of the 5th International Semantic Web Conference*, 2006.

[23] Cheskin and S. Archetype/Sapient, "Ecommerce trust: Building trust in digital environments," 1999.

[24] P. A. Chirita, S. Idreos, M. Koubarakis, and W. Nejdl, "Publish/subscribe for rdf-based p2p networks," in *Proceedings of 1st European Semantic Web Symposium*, 2004.

[25] Y.-H. Chu, J. Feigenbaum, B. LaMacchia, P. Resnick, and M. Strauss, "REFEREE: Trust management for Web applications," *Computer Networks and ISDN Systems*, vol. 29, no. 8–13, pp. 953–964, 1997.
[26] K. Cook, *Trust in Society.* Russell Sage Foundation, 2001.
[27] F. Cornelli, E. Damiani, S. D. C. di Vimercati, S. Paraboschi, and P. Samarati, "Choosing reputable servents in a p2p network," in *WWW '02: Proceedings of the 11th International Conference on World Wide Web*, pp. 376–386, New York, NY, USA: ACM Press, 2002.
[28] C. L. Corritore, B. Kracher, and S. Wiedenbeck, "On-line trust: Concepts, evolving themes, a model," *International Journal of Human-Computer Studies*, vol. 58, no. 6, pp. 737–758, 2003.
[29] E. Damiani, D. C. di Vimercati, S. Paraboschi, P. Samarati, and F. Violante, "A reputation-based approach for choosing reliable resources in peer-to-peer networks," in *CCS '02: Proceedings of the 9th ACM Conference on Computer and Communications Security*, pp. 207–216, New York, NY, USA: ACM Press, 2002.
[30] I. Davis and E. Viiello, "Relationship: A vocabulary for describing relationships between people," 2004.
[31] Y. Diao, S. Rizvi, and M. Franklin, "Towards *an internet*-scale xml dissemination service," in *Proceedings of VLDB2004, August 2004.*
[32] B. Dragovic, E. Kotsovinos, S. Hand, and P. R. Pietzuch, "Xenotrust: Event-based distributed trust management," in *DEXA '03: Proceedings of the 14th International Workshop on Database and Expert Systems Applications*, p. 410, Washington, DC, USA: IEEE Computer Society, 2003.
[33] E. Dumbill, "Finding friends with xml and rdf," 2002.
[34] R. Falcone and C. Castelfranchi, "Social trust: A cognitive approach," pp. 55–90, 2001.
[35] B. J. Fogg, J. Marshall, O. Laraki, A. Osipovich, C. Varma, N. Fang, J. Paul, A. Rangnekar, J. Shon, P. Swani, and M. Treinen, "What makes web sites credible?: A report on a large quantitative study," in *CHI '01: Proceedings of the SIGCHI Conference on Human Factors in Computing Systems*, pp. 61–68, New York, NY, USA: ACM Press, 2001.
[36] J. Futrelle and J. Myers, "Tracking provenance semantics in heterogeneous execution systems," *Concurrency and Computation: Practice and Experience*, 2007.
[37] M. Garden and G. Dudek, "Semantic feedback for hybrid recommendations in recommendz," in *Proceedings of the IEEE International Conference on e-Technology, e-Commerce, and e-Service (EEE05)*, 2005.
[38] Y. Gil and V. Ratnakar, "Trusting information sources one citizen at a time," in *Proceedings of the First International Semantic Web Conference*, June 2002.
[39] J. Golbeck, *Computing and applying trust in web-based social networks.* PhD thesis, University of Maryland, College Park, MD, April 2005.
[40] J. Golbeck, "Generating predictive movie recommendations from trust in social networks," in *Proceedings of the Fourth International Conference on Trust Management*, 2006.

[41] J. Golbeck, "Trust and nuanced profile similarity in online social networks," in MINDSWAP Technical Report TR-MS1284, 2006.

[42] J. Golbeck, "The dynamics of web-based social networks: Membership, relationships, and change," *First Monday*, vol. 12, no. 11, 2007.

[43] J. Golbeck and C. Halaschek-Wiener, "Trust-based revision for expressive web syndication," Tech. Rep. MINDSWAP TR-MS1293, University of Maryland, College Park, 2007.

[44] J. Golbeck and J. Hendler, "Reputation network analysis for email filtering," in *Proceedings of the First Conference on Email and Anti-Spam*, 2004.

[45] J. Golbeck and J. Hendler, "A semantic web approach to tracking provenance in scientific workflows," *Concurrency and Computation: Practice and Experience*, vol. in this issue, 2007.

[46] J. Golbeck and B. Parsia, "Trust network-based filtering of aggregated claims," *International Journal of Metadata, Semantics, and Ontologies*, vol. 1, no. 1, pp. 58–65, 2006.

[47] J. Golbeck, B. Parsia, and J. Hendler, "Trust networks on the semantic web," in *Proceedings of Cooperative Intelligent Agents*, 2003.

[48] T. Grandison and M. Sloman, "A survey of trust in internet application," *IEEE Communications Surveys and Tutorials*, vol. 3, no. 4, 2000.

[49] E. Gray, J. Seigneur, Y. Chen, and C. Jensen, "Trust propagation in small worlds," in *Proceedings of the First International Conference on Trust Management*, 2003.

[50] R. Guha, R. Kumar, P. Raghavan, and A. Tomkins, "Propagation of trust and distrust," in *WWW '04: Proceedings of the 13th International Conference on World Wide Web*, pp. 403–412, New York, NY, USA: ACM Press, 2004.

[51] V. Haarslev and R. Møller, "Incremental query answering for implementing document retrieval services," in *Proceeding of the International Workshop on Description Logics*, 2003.

[52] C. Halaschek-Wiener, *Expressive Syndication on the Web Using a Description Logic Approach*. PhD thesis, University of Maryland, College Park, MD, USA, November 2007.

[53] R. Hardin, *Trust and Trustworthiness*. Russell Sage Foundation, 2002.

[54] J. L. Herlocker, J. A. Konstan, and J. Riedl, "Explaining collaborative filtering recommendations," in *Proceedings of the 2000 ACM Conference on Computer Supported Cooperative Work*, pp. 241–250, 2000.

[55] J. L. Herlocker, J. A. Konstan, L. G. Terveen, and J. T. Riedl, "Evaluating collaborative filtering recommender systems," *ACM Transactions on Information Systems (TOIS)*, vol. 22, pp. 5–53, 2004.

[56] C. M. Jonker and J. Treur, "Formal analysis of models for the dynamics of trust based on experiences," in *MAAMAW '99: Proceedings of the 9th European Workshop on Modelling Autonomous Agents in a Multi-Agent World*, pp. 221–231, London, UK: Springer-Verlag, 1999.

[57] A. Jøsang, "The right type of trust for distributed systems," in *NSPW '96: Proceedings of the 1996 Workshop on New Security Paradigms*, pp. 119–131, 1996.

[58] A. Jøsang, R. Hayward, and S. Pope, "Trust network analysis with subjective logic," in *ACSC '06: Proceedings of the 29th Australasian Computer Science Conference*, pp. 85–94, Darlinghurst, Australia: Australian Computer Society, Inc., 2006.

[59] A. Jøsang, C. Keser, and T. Dimitrakos, "Can we manage trust?," in *iTrust*, pp. 93–107, 2005.

[60] L. Kagal, T. Finin, and Y. Peng, "A framework for distributed trust management," in *Workshop on Autonomy, Delegation and Control, 2001.*

[61] S. D. Kamvar, M. T. Schlosser, and H. Garcia-Molina, "The eigentrust algorithm for reputation management in p2p networks," in *WWW '03: Proceedings of the 12th International Conference on World Wide Web*, pp. 640–651, New York, NY, USA: ACM Press, 2003.

[62] S. Kent and R. Atkinson, "Security architecture for the internet protocol," 1998.

[63] R. Khare and A. Rifkin, "Weaving a web of trust," *World Wide Web Journal*, vol. 2, no. 3, pp. 77–112, 1997.

[64] R. Khare and A. Rifkin, "Trust management on the world wide web," *First Monday*, vol. 10, no. 7, 2006.

[65] J. Kim, E. Deelman, Y. Gil, G. Mehta, and V. Ratnakar, "Provenance trails in the wings/pegasus system," *Concurrency and Computation: Practice and Experience*, 2007.

[66] V. Kolovski, J. Hendler, and B. Parsia, "Analyzing web access control policies," in *WWW '07: Proceedings of the 16th international conference on World Wide Web*, pp. 677–686, New York, NY, USA: ACM Press, 2007.

[67] V. Kolovski, B. Parsia, Y. Katz, and J. A. Hendler, "Representing web service policies in owl-dl," in *International Semantic Web Conference*, pp. 461–475, 2005.

[68] J. A. Konstan, B. N. Miller, D. Maltz, J. L. Herlocker, L. R. Gordon, and J. Riedl, "Grouplens: Applying collaborative filtering to usenet news," *Communications of the ACM*, vol. 40, no. 3, pp. 77–87, 1997.

[69] E. Kotsovinos and A. Williams, "Bambootrust: Practical scalable trust management for global public computing," in *SAC '06: Proceedings of the 2006 ACM Symposium on Applied computing*, pp. 1893–1897, New York, NY, USA: ACM, 2006.

[70] U. Kuter and J. Golbeck, "Sunny: A new algorithm for trust inference in social networks, using probabilistic confidence models," in *Proceedings of the National Conference on Artificial Intelligence (AAAI)*, 2007.

[71] Y. Lashkari, M. Metral, and P. Maes, "Collaborative interface agents," in *Proceedings of the Twelfth National Conference on Artificial Intelligence*, pp. 444–449, 1994.

[72] T. Leithead, W. Nejdl, D. Olmedilla, K. Seamons, M. Winslett, T. Yu, and C. C. Zhang, "How to Exploit Ontologies for Trust Negotiation," in *Proceedings of Workshop on Trust, Security and Reputation on the Semantic Web in Conjunction with the 3rd International Semantic Web Conference*, Hiroshima, Japan (7th–11th November 2004), The Japanese Society for Artificial Intelligence and The Semantic Web Science Association, 2004.

[73] R. Levien and A. Aiken, "Attack-resistant trust metrics for public key certification," in *7th USENIX Security Symposium*, pp. 229–242, 1998.
[74] L. Li and I. Horrocks, "A software framework for matchmaking based on semantic web technology," in *Proceedings of the 12th International World Wide Web Conference*, 2003.
[75] M. Lorch, S. Proctor, R. Lepro, D. Kafura, and S. Shah, "First experiences using xacml for access control in distributed systems," in *ACM Workshop on XML Security*, 2003.
[76] C. A. Lynch, "When documents deceive: Trust and provenance as new factors for information retrieval in a tangled web," *Journal of American Society for Information Science and Technology*, vol. 52, no. 1, pp. 12–17, 2001.
[77] P. Maes, "Agents that reduce work and information overload," *Communications of the ACM*, vol. 37, no. 7, pp. 30–40, 1994.
[78] S. Marti, *Trust and Reputation in Peer to Peer Networks*. PhD thesis, Stanford University, May 2005.
[79] P. Massa and P. Avesani, "Trust-aware collaborative filtering for recommender systems," in *Proceeding of Federated International Conference On The Move to Meaningful Internet: CoopIS, DOA, ODBASE*, 2004.
[80] P. Massa and B. Bhattacharjee, "Using trust in recommender systems: An experimental analysis," in *Proceedings of 2nd International Conference on Trust Management*, 2004.
[81] R. Matthew, R. Agrawal, and P. Domingos, "Trust management for the semantic web," in *Proceedings of the Second International Semantic Web Conference*, 2003.
[82] K. A. McCabe, M. L. Rigdon, and V. L. Smith, "Positive reciprocity and intentions in trust games," *Journal of Economic Behavior and Organization*, vol. 52, pp. 267–275, October 2003.
[83] B. N. Miller, I. Albert, S. K. Lam, J. A. Konstan, and J. Riedl, "Movielens unplugged: Experiences with an occasionally connected recommender system," in *IUI '03: Proceedings of the 8th International Conference on Intelligent User Interfaces*, pp. 263–266, New York, NY, USA: ACM, 2003.
[84] L. Moreau, B. Ludäscher, I. Altintas, R. S. Barga, S. Bowers, S. Callahan, G. Chin Jr., B. Clifford, S. Cohen, S. Cohen-Boulakia, S. Davidson, E. Deelman, L. Digiampietri, I. Foster, J. Freire, J. Frew, J. Futrelle, T. Gibson, Y. Gil, C. Goble, J. Golbeck, P. Groth, D. A. Holland, S. Jiang, J. Kim, D. Koop, A. Krenek, T. McPhillips, G. Mehta, S. Miles, D. Metzger, S. Munroe, J. Myers, B. Plale, N. Podhorszki, V. Ratnakar, E. Santos, C. Scheidegger, K. Schuchardt, M. Seltzer, Y. L. Simmhan, C. Silva, P. Slaughter, E. Stephan, R. Stevens, D. Turi, H. Vo, M. Wilde, J. Zhao, and Y. Zhao, "The first provenance challenge," *Concurrency and Computation: Practice and Experience*, 2007.
[85] W. Nejdl, D. Olmedilla, and M. Winslett, "Peertrust: Automated trust negotiation for peers on the semantic web," in Technical Report, 2003.
[86] J. O'Donovan and B. Smyth, "Trust in recommender systems," in *IUI '05: Proceedings of the 10th International Conference on Intelligent User Interfaces*, pp. 167–174, New York, NY, USA: ACM, 2005.

[87] B. Oki, M. Pfluegl, and D. Skeen, "The information bus: An architecture for extensible distributed systems," in *Proceedings of the 14th SOSP*, 1993.

[88] L. Page, S. Brin, R. Motwani, and T. Winograd, "The pagerank citation ranking: Bringing order to the web," Tech. Rep., Stanford Digital Library Technologies Project, 1998.

[89] P. Perny and J. D. Zucker, "Preference-based search and machine learning for collaborative filtering: The "film-conseil" recommender system," *Information, Interaction , Intelligence*, vol. 1, no. 1, pp. 9–48, 2001.

[90] J. Riegelsberger, M. A. Sasse, and J. D. McCarthy, "Shiny happy people building trust?: Photos on e-commerce websites and consumer trust," in *CHI '03: Proceedings of the SIGCHI Conference on Human Factors in Computing Systems*, pp. 121–128, New York, NY, USA: ACM, 2003.

[91] A. Salam, L. Iyer, P. Palvia, and R. Singh, "Trust in e-commerce," *Communications of the ACM*, vol. 48, no. 2, pp. 72–77, 2005.

[92] M. C. Schraefel, N. R. Shadbolt, N. Gibbins, S. Harris, and H. Glaser, "Cs aktive space: Representing computer science in the semantic web," in *WWW '04: Proceedings of the 13th International Conference on World Wide Web*, pp. 384–392, New York, NY, USA: ACM, 2004.

[93] M. C. Schraefel, M. Wilson, A. Russell, and D. A. Smith, "Mspace: Improving information access to multimedia domains with multimodal exploratory search," *Communications of the ACM*, vol. 49, no. 4, pp. 47–49, 2006.

[94] J. Seigneur, N. Dimmock, C. Bryce, and C. D. Jensen, "Combating spam with {TEA} (trusted email addresses)," in *Second Annual Conference on Privacy, Security and Trust*, New Brunswick, Canada, October 2004.

[95] N. Shankar and W. Arbaugh, "On trust for ubiquitous computing," in *Workshop on Security in Ubiquitous Computing*, 2002.

[96] R. Sherwood, S. Lee, and B. Bhattacharjee, "Cooperative peer groups in nice," in *Proceedings of IEEE INFOCOM*, 2003.

[97] R. Sinha and K. Swearingen, "Comparing recommendations made by online systems and friends.," in *Proceedings of the DELOS-NSF Workshop on Personalization and Recommender Systems in Digital Libraries*, 2001.

[98] H. Skogsrud, B. Benatallah, and F. Casati, "Model-driven trust negotiation for web services," *IEEE Internet Computing*, vol. 7, no. 6, pp. 45–52, 2003.

[99] C. V. Slyke, F. Belanger, and C. L. Comunale, "Factors influencing the adoption of web-based shopping: The impact of trust," *SIGMIS Database*, vol. 35, no. 2, pp. 32–49, 2004.

[100] I. Stoica, R. Morris, D. Liben-Nowell, D. R. Karger, F. F. Kaashoek, F. Dabek, and H. Balakrishnan, "Chord: A scalable peer-to-peer lookup protocol for internet applications," *IEEE/ACM Transactions on Networking*, vol. 11, 2003.

[101] K. Swearingen and R. Sinha, "Beyond algorithms: An hci perspective on recommender systems," in *Proceedings of the ACM SIGIR 2001 Workshop on Recommender Systems*, 2001.

[102] M. Uschold, P. Clark, F. Dickey, C. Fung, S. Smith, S. U. M. Wilke, S. Bechhofer, and I. Horrocks, "A semantic infosphere," in *Proceedings of the International Semantic Web Conference*, 2003.

[103] A. S. Vedamuthu, D. Orchard, F. Hirsch, M. Hondo, P. Yendluri, T. Boubez, and M. Yalinalp, "Web services policy 1.5 — framework," http://www.w3.org/TR/ws-policy, 04 September 2007.

[104] D. S. Wallach, D. Balfanz, D. Dean, and E. W. Felten, "Extensible security architectures for java," in *SOSP '97: Proceedings of the Sixteenth ACM Symposium on Operating Systems Principles*, pp. 116–128, New York, NY, USA: ACM Press, 1997.

[105] J. Wang, B. Jin, and J. Li, "An ontology-based publish/subscribe system," in *Middleware*, 2004.

[106] Y. Wang and J. Vassileva, "Trust and reputation model in peer-to-peer networks," in *Proceedings of IEEE Conference on P2P Computing*, pp. 150–157, September 2003.

[107] M. Wilson, A. Russell, M. C. Schraefel, and D. A. Smith, "Mspace mobile: A ui gestalt to support on-the-go info-interaction," in *CHI '06: CHI '06 Extended Abstracts on Human Factors in Computing Systems*, pp. 247–250, New York, NY, USA: ACM, 2006.

[108] M. Winslett, T. Yu, K. E. Seamons, A. Hess, J. Jacobson, R. Jarvis, B. Smith, and L. Yu, "Negotiating trust on the web," *IEEE Internet Computing*, vol. 6, no. 6, pp. 30–37, 2002.

[109] Y. Yang, Y. Hu, and J. Chen, "A web trust-inducing model for e-commerce and empirical research," in *ICEC '05: Proceedings of the 7th International Conference on Electronic Commerce*, pp. 188–194, New York, NY, USA: ACM, 2005.

[110] I. Yaniv and E. Kleinberger, "Advice taking in decision making: Egocentric discounting and reputation formation," *Organizational Behavior and Human Decision Processes*, vol. 83, no. 2, pp. 260–281, 2000.

[111] B. Yu and M. P. Singh, "A social mechanism of reputation management in electronic communities," in *CIA '00: Proceedings of the 4th International Workshop on Cooperative Information Agents IV, The Future of Information Agents in Cyberspace*, pp. 154–165, London, UK: Springer-Verlag, 2000.

[112] J. Zhao, C. Goble, R. Stevens, and D. Turi, "Mining taverna's semantic web of provenance," *Concurrency and Computation: Practice and Experience*, 2007.

[113] J. Zhao, C. Wroe, C. A. Goble, R. Stevens, D. Quan, and R. M. Greenwood, "Using semantic web technologies for representing e-science provenance," in *International Semantic Web Conference*, pp. 92–106, 2004.

[114] C.-N. Ziegler and J. Golbeck, "Investigating correlations of trust and interest similarity," *Decision Support Services*, p. 1, 2006.

[115] C.-N. Ziegler and G. Lausen, "Analyzing correlation between trust and user similarity in online communities," in *Proceedings of the Second International Conference on Trust Management*, 2004.

[116] C.-N. Ziegler and G. Lausen, "Spreading activation models for trust propagation," in *Proceedings of the IEEE International Conference on e-Technology, e-Commerce, and e-Service*, Taipei, Taiwan: IEEE Computer Society Press, March 2004.

Lightning Source UK Ltd.
Milton Keynes UK
UKOW06f0430081215

264315UK00003B/123/P

9 781601 981165